"Dick Tibbits has written a helpful guide to the difficult task of forgiving. He writes with a deep understanding of the subject and offers a methodology that will certainly work for those who apply its principles."

> — FRED LUSKIN, PH.D.; Director and Cofounder of the Stanford Forgiveness Project; author of *Forgive for Good* and *Stress Free for Good*

"Forgiveness is more than a noble gesture toward someone else. It is an act of kindness that changes one's self and the world as well. In a world seething with a thousand hatreds, what could be more important?"

> — LARRY DOSSEY, M.D.; author of *Healing Words, Prayer Is Good Medicine* and *The Extraordinary Healing Power of Ordinary Things*

"Dr. Tibbits has done the research and scientifically documented the healing power of forgiveness. Read it and live!"

> — HAROLD G. KOENIG, M.D.; Associate Professor of Psychiatry and Medicine, Duke University Medical Center; author of *The Healing Power of Faith*

"*Forgive to Live* is so timely and relevant because the wisdom transcends barriers of age, race, social status and spiritual background. Literally, the ideas and practices in *Forgive to Live* may save your life."

> — KENNETH R. PELLETIER, Ph.D., M.D.; Clinical Professor of Medicine, University of Arizona School of Medicine and University of California School of Medicine, San Francisco; author of *The Best of Alternative Medicine* and *Sound Mind, Sound Body*

"*Forgive to Live* is outstanding because it takes you through each vital step of the forgiveness process. It's a compelling read. Once you've finished the book you'll want to pass it on to everyone!"

> — SCOTT BRADY, M.D.; Founder and Director of the Brady Institute for Health; author of *Pain Free for Life*

"Perhaps the reason that you have not been able to forgive is because you have the wrong impression of what forgiveness is. Dr. Tibbits finally exposes the myths of forgiveness and offers vital answers to those of us struggling to forgive."

> — NICK HALL, PH.D.; author of *Change Your Beliefs, Change Your Life*

"We all have a grievance story. Who hasn't been hurt? Who hasn't struggled with forgiveness? We all need this book!"

> — MONICA REED, M.D.; C.E.O., Celebration Health; author of *The Creation Health Breakthrough*

"In this inspiring and thoughtful book, Dr. Dick Tibbits presents a compelling portrait of a 'muscular' forgiveness with the reminder that strong people forgive. Forgiveness is vital to good health—both physical and mental. This book could not come at a better time in a world that has become increasingly harsh and unforgiving. It's a mandatory read for all health-care professionals and their patients."

> — JAMES M. RIPPE, M.D.; Associate Professor of Medicine (Cardiology), Tufts University School of Medicine; Founder and Director of the Rippe Lifestyle Institute; author of *Fit Over Forty* and *Fit for Success*

FORGIVE
TO
LIVE

HOW FORGIVENESS CAN
SAVE YOUR LIFE

DR. DICK TIBBITS
WITH STEVE HALLIDAY

THOMAS NELSON
Since 1798

FORGIVE TO LIVE

Published by Thomas Nelson Publishers
501 Nelson Place Nashville, TN 37214

HELPING PEOPLE WORLDWIDE EXPERIENCE *the* MANIFEST PRESENCE *of* GOD

PUBLISHER'S NOTE: This book is not intended to replace a one-on-one relationship with a qualified health-care professional, but as a sharing of knowledge and information from the research and experience of the author. You are advised and encouraged to consult with your health-care professional in all matters relating to your health and the health of your family. The publisher and author disclaim any liability arising directly or indirectly from the use of this book.

AUTHOR'S NOTE: This book contains numerous case histories and patient stories. In order to preserve the privacy of the people involved, I have disguised their names, appearances, and aspects of their personal stories so that they are not identifiable. Case histories may also include composite characters.

General Editor, Florida Hospital: Todd Chobotar
Florida Hospital Review Board: James Rippe, MD, John McVay, DMin, Dick Duerksen
Photography: Spencer Freeman
Illustrations by: Red Hughes
Cover Design by: Russ McIntosh, Brand Navigation, LLC, www.brandnavigation.com
Interior Design by: Rainbow Graphics

Published in association with the literary agency of Alive Communications, Inc., 7680 Goddard St, Suite 200, Colorado Springs, CO 80920.

Library of Congress Cataloging-in-Publication Data

Tibbits, Dick.
 Forgive to live : how forgiveness can save your life /
Dick Tibbits with Steve Halliday.
  p. cm.
 Summary: "Clinically proven steps and tools every person needs to uncover their grievance story, eliminate the unresolved anger that they can and can't see--and forgive for good"--Provided by publisher.
 Includes bibliographical references.
 ISBN-13: 978-0-7852-9725-3

 1. Forgiveness--Religious aspects--Christianity.   I. Halliday, Steve, 1957- II. Title.
 BV4647.F55T53 2006
 158.2--dc22

2006014163

Printed in the United States of America
06 07 08 09 10 BVG 9 8 7 6 5 4 3 2 1

BOOKS BY DR. DICK TIBBITS
Forgive to Live
Forgive to Live Workbook
Forgive to Live Devotional

ALSO BY DR. DICK TIBBITS
Forgive to Live Video Curriculum

To my wife Arta.
The person who has lived with me longest,
and had opportunity to forgive me most,
I dedicate this book to you.

CONTENTS

ACKNOWLEDGMENTS

I want to sincerely thank those who have shaped my life and those who have contributed to the completion of this book. There are more of you than I could possibly acknowledge. This book's very existence is the culmination of the friendship and support of many individuals who have impacted my professional and personal journey. I am profoundly grateful to each of you.

First I want to thank my parents, Henry and Bev Tibbits, who were willing to forgive me often for all the antics I managed to pull off as a teenager.

Then to Stu Jayne, Larry Yeagley, O. G. Phillips, and Al Brendel, thanks for impacting my lifelong career as a caregiver.

I want to thank Todd Chobotar and my agent Lee Hough for their enthusiasm and persistence in getting this book to market.

I also want to thank Don Jernigan, Lars Houmann, Des Cummings, Brian Paradis, and the leadership team at Florida Hospital for their vision of publishing books on whole-person health.

Thanks go to Ken Pelletier and Fred Luskin for your support and your willingness to think outside the box. You inspired me to reach beyond what *is*, toward what can be.

To the whole team at Integrity Publishers, and especially Joey Paul, thanks for believing in the message of this book and making it all possible. Thanks go to my editor Lisa Guest. This book is much stronger because of your efforts.

And of course thanks to Steve Halliday. I am especially grateful for your ability to take my words and thoughts and give them life on the page.

FOREWORD

When was the last time you said "I forgive you" and really meant it?

Forgive to Live is so timely and relevant because the wisdom transcends barriers of age, race, social status, and spiritual background. Who among us hasn't been hurt? From the youngest girl to the oldest man we have all experienced hurt at the hands of others. In response, anger, grievance, and revenge are all too frequently the universal result.

By reading this book you embark on a journey into territory many people have yet to explore. You have taken the first step in unlocking the mysteries and benefits of forgiveness.

Forgiveness is no easy task, and Dr. Dick Tibbits should know. He lived it and experienced it long before he wrote about it. But what makes *Forgive to Live* unique is that Dr. Tibbits, in conjunction with Florida Hospital and the Stanford University School of Medicine, conducted a research study demonstrating the effects of anger and forgiveness on your health. By identifying the steps necessary to forgive, he opened the path for everyone to experience a longer, healthier life through the healing power of forgiveness.

When I first met Dick, it was in my role as an advisor to Disney. I was asked to help Disney assess the competing applications from various hospitals for building and designing an innovative health-care delivery system at Disney's new community, called Celebration, adjacent to Disney World. As I became acquainted with Dick's work, I realized that he had a passion for the integration of mind/body/spirit medicine, and given that I did as well, we formed a natural collegial relationship. During our work with Disney, Dick and I both served on the board of the Center for Health Futures. In that role we had the privilege of reviewing some of the best forward-thinking ideas in health-care, with an eye toward how those ideas could be applied in a practical way in a hospital setting at Celebration, Florida.

It was also my privilege to introduce Dick to another colleague of mine, Dr. Fred Luskin, who was a post-doctoral Fellow at the Stanford University School of Medicine where I was Clinical Professor of Medicine. At that time, I knew both Dick and Fred were interested in forgiveness as an approach to healing. Fred was focusing primarily on the psychological and psychosocial benefits of forgiveness, and Dick was primarily interested in the health and spiritual benefits that forgiveness provided. When those two creative minds got together, I knew the field of forgiveness would be significantly advanced.

Dick's research demonstrated that forgiveness is an effective approach for assisting some individuals with high blood pressure and elevated anger in managing their conditions. When forgiveness was learned and practiced over an eight-week period, clinically significant reductions of blood pressure as well as anger were achieved. This made sense to me because I knew that my colleague and friend Dr. Redford Williams at the Duke Medical School had demonstrated how anger was related to heart disease, and Fred Luskin had shown how learning forgiveness reduced anger. Dick's unique contribution was in closing the loop and demonstrating how forgiveness could lower blood pressure by reducing anger and hostility.

What is especially helpful in Dick's work is the practical, straightforward advice he offers on how to forgive. The steps to forgiveness he offers make sense and are easy to understand and apply. Even if you do not suffer from high blood pressure, I would encourage you to learn and practice forgiveness. By doing so you will discover how much your life can change for the better. Forgiveness as Dick defines it will free you from your past hurts, thus allowing you to have the energy and focus to pursue your dreams. Literally, the ideas and practices in *Forgive to Live* may save your life.

In *Forgive to Live* Dick Tibbits provides many powerful illustrations of how choosing not to forgive hurts you more than it helps you. Actually, the truth is that every time we lash out at someone who has hurt us (either outwardly or by fantasizing about it inwardly), we reopen the wound and hurt mainly ourselves.

Remember your childhood years of dealing with hurt at school? "Tell Susan you're sorry!" the teacher would say. "Sorry!" you reply in an annoyed grunt. "Tell Tommy you forgive him," your teacher would chime. "I forgive you," you reply, still in tears. Now where is the justice in that? Tommy isn't really sorry and you didn't really forgive him. He's still a bully and you're still a victim. For the rest of the third grade you laid in wait for revenge! Sound familiar? This is the same principle that most of us carry into adolescence and well into adulthood. Unfortunately some people carry this same method into death and do not live half the life that they could have.

Most books about forgiveness outline the importance of it and why you should do it. But after you have read the book and you are eager to get started, you realize that something is missing. You know why you should forgive, and the benefits are outstanding, but how do you get there? You might try taking your own steps, and hopefully they work, but most times they do not. It's like being trapped in a maze where everyone is telling you to get out but there are no directions. That's why I believe *Forgive to Live* is so unique. It does not simply tell you that you should forgive, which we have all heard time and time again, but it gives you the scientifically verified steps of *how* to forgive.

Still wondering if this book is for you? Try this. Think of the last person who really hurt you, or a person with whom you had a big confrontation and they made you angry. Think of that situation in your life where you felt like things were out of control. Who is the villain in the scene? Who won? Who lost? Can you think of anything you wish you had said or done? Can you think of some vengeful act that would really "stick it to them" so that they would know how it felt to be in your shoes? If you are being flooded with strong emotions, you are reliving your grievance story and you have not forgiven—and this book is for you. The good news is that you can reframe that situation to have a positive result—one in which you win.

There are three great reasons to read this book. First, it's important to remember that if you ignore pain, it does not go away. So in one way or another you're going to have to deal with it. This book takes you through that process. Second, for once this book is really about you and what you can do. When you forgive, you are triumphant. It is not about getting your offender back but about releasing yourself from the stronghold of pain and the desire for revenge. Dr. Tibbits shows you how. Third, this book outlines the practical steps you can take to forgive and gain a broader perspective on the best way to live your life.

This is why *Forgive to Live* is such a perfect title: it says it all. Not forgive to lose, or forgive to die peacefully, but *Forgive to Live*!

Kenneth R. Pelletier, PhD, MD(hc)
Clinical Professor of Medicine
University of Arizona School of Medicine
and University of California School of Medicine (UCSF), San Francisco

INTRODUCTION

HOW FORGIVENESS CAN SAVE YOUR LIFE

"I f you don't do something right away, you could die."

Several hours after his unsettling doctor's appointment, Les still felt shaken by the ominous words that continued to ring in his ears: *You could die.* His thoughts raced back to his father, who had died at age forty-seven from heart disease. He grimly noted his own blood pressure, already measuring an alarming 154/102—and climbing. Would he follow his dad's footsteps to an early grave?

Les's stressful job—"rush, rush, rush," as he summed it up—didn't help matters. He felt even more pressure when his recent promotion to supervisor encouraged the men and women under him to use their friendship to ask for frequent favors. They didn't like it when Les refused many of their requests, and soon he began to hear through the grapevine many of the nasty comments they were making about him behind his back. This backstabbing made Les angry—although he never called his emotions that. He didn't see himself as angry. After all, he was not an explosive person, and he didn't easily lose his temper. Even so, the test results his doctor had just gone over with Les indicated that he harbored a high degree of resentment and inner bitterness. Apparently, rather than showing his true feelings, Les had simply learned to stuff them.

For all of these reasons, Les knew he was in trouble—but what could he do?

Fortunately, his physician had an idea. "Would you be open to taking part in a study that teaches participants who suffer from high blood pressure a new way of managing their disease?" he asked. Les decided he had nothing to lose, so he joined the eight-week forgiveness training program I had designed.

Within two months, Les's blood pressure dropped back to a normal reading of 120/80, and his anger scores fell well within the normal range. He felt as though he had reclaimed his future. Forgiveness had literally saved his life.

While Les's story may be more dramatic than most, it is just one of hundreds of accounts of ordinary men and women who have discovered the healing power of forgiveness. In this book I will clearly unpack for you the same principles I taught Les and the other participants in my study so that you, too, can *Forgive to Live*.

IDENTIFYING THE REAL PROBLEM

"But I've tried forgiveness," you say, "and it didn't work for me." May I suggest that the problem may not be forgiveness itself, but your understanding of forgiveness? In fact, I'd be willing to bet that your struggle with forgiveness not "working" for you has a lot in common with the trouble I once had with a stubborn bolt.

No matter how hard I tried—determined teenager that I was—I could not loosen that bolt. Perhaps it had rusted? To test my theory, I poured some Liquid Wrench on the threads—but still it would not budge. Then I retrieved a large wrench that could provide a great deal of leverage. Still the bolt refused to move. Clearly, more drastic measures were needed. So I lit a torch and heated the bolt—*and still no luck!* No matter how hard I tried to loosen it, the bolt continued to hold fast.

When I reported my frustrating dilemma to my father, he simply laughed.

"Don't you know that's a left-handed thread?" he asked. "In order for it to come off, you have to turn it as though you were *tightening* a normal bolt."

It had never occurred to me that I had to do just the opposite of what I thought would work. Sure enough, when I followed my dad's advice, the bolt quickly came free.

I've discovered that the process of forgiveness can be an awful lot like my frustrating experience with that stubborn bolt. We try so hard to forgive, we try to forgive so often, and we try to forgive in so many ways, yet nothing seems to work. But you know what? In every case of failed forgiveness I've observed, the problem lies in a faulty understanding of forgiveness. We try to loosen a left-threaded bolt by using a right-handed solution.

If forgiveness just hasn't "worked" for you, could it be that you've been going about it the wrong way? Maybe you've mistaken the real thing for a widely accepted—but totally flawed—substitute.

What Forgiveness Is Not

Let's briefly consider a few problematic ideas that cause confusion because they misrepresent the true nature of forgiveness.

1. Forgive and forget

Some people believe that if you have not been able to forget some unpleasant event, then you must not have forgiven either the act or the one who acted against you. This idea could not be further from the truth, for if it were true, then only those individuals with memory loss would be able to forgive. The fact is, when something is important to you, you *will* remember it. Forgiveness does not wipe out your memory, nor is it a delete key for reality. The test of genuine forgiveness is not *whether* you remember the event in question, but *how* you remember it.

2. Forgiveness that implies "It's OK"

Can a wrong committed against you ever be right? Of course not. Wrong is wrong even when it's forgiven. Forgiveness never makes a wrong act right, nor does forgiveness condone or excuse the wrong act. Forgiveness defines who you are; it does not redefine the other's wrongful act as right.

3. Forgive and make up

Often forgiveness can lead to reconciliation, but not always. It takes two people to reconcile, but only one to forgive. Even if the other party refuses to participate in forgiveness, your ability to forgive remains unhindered. You can forgive whether or not the other person is involved.

4. Forgive and set others free

Certainly forgiveness can involve pardon—but it doesn't have to. You can forgive people and still hold them accountable for the legal and natural consequences of their actions. Forgiveness does not suspend the law of cause and effect. What changes is your desire for vengeance and retaliation, and that change helps you avoid an escalation of attacks and counterattacks. Forgiveness frees *you*.

So if forgiveness is not pardoning, condoning, excusing, forgetting, denying, or even reconciling, then what is it? How can genuine forgiveness best be defined so that it can do its amazing work of healing in your life?

WHAT FORGIVENESS IS

In light of all the misconceptions, I find it interesting that no single definition of forgiveness has become universally accepted. Consider just a few definitions, some of which I like for their humor and others for their insight.

- Forgiveness is the feeling of peace that emerges as you take your hurt less personally, take responsibility for how you feel, and become a hero instead of a victim in the story you tell. . . . Forgiveness means that even though you are wounded, you choose to hurt and suffer less.—*Fred Luskin*

- Forgiveness is giving up my right to hurt you for hurting me. —*Unknown*

- Our friends are those who know their own faults well enough to forgive ours.—*Moulton Farnham*

- Always forgive your enemies; nothing annoys them so much. —*Oscar Wilde*

- He who cannot forgive others breaks the bridge over which he himself must travel.—*George Herbert*

- Forgiveness can almost be considered a selfish act because of all the benefits received by the one who forgives.—*Unknown*

I like many aspects of what these individuals have said about forgiveness, but here's the definition I will use in this book:

Forgiveness is the process of reframing one's anger and hurt from the past, with the goal of recovering one's peace in the present and revitalizing one's purpose and hopes for the future.

THE THREE PHASES OF FORGIVENESS

When you take apart my definition of forgiveness, you'll quickly note that its practice can be divided into three distinct phases:

- Phase 1: How I handle the memories of painful things said and done to me in the past

- Phase 2: How I overcome the negative emotions I feel right now

- Phase 3: How I free myself from a hurtful past to achieve my desired future

This book will help you understand and practice these necessary steps of forgiving. Without covering the full range of past, present, and future, your forgiveness will be incomplete, making it much more difficult for you to experience a full and satisfying life.

Before we get started, I want to acknowledge that my work builds on the insights of a few pioneers. Twenty years ago, Lewis Smedes published his landmark book *Forgive & Forget*. Smedes was the first to place forgiveness into the mainstream as a topic for scientific consideration. A decade later Dr. Redford Williams published his own best-selling book *Anger Kills*, in which he proved that repressed anger can in fact kill. He listed seventeen strategies for controlling hostile feelings, and forgiveness was one of the options. But Williams offered no specific steps on how to forgive, nor did he clinically verify how practicing forgiveness could improve one's health. Most recently, Fred Luskin encouraged his own readers to *Forgive for Good*. Luskin successfully demonstrated that the practice of forgiveness can measurably reduce anger.

I have attempted to take the science of forgiveness to the next level by teaching specific steps—backed by clinical research—that will reduce the serious health risks associated with repressed anger and hostility. I began with the premise that if anger kills and if forgiveness reduces anger, then forgiveness could be used as an effective clinical intervention to reduce high blood pressure. *Forgive to Live* demonstrates that practicing forgiveness can save your life.

THREE DIMENSIONS OF FORGIVENESS

Forgiveness is not an emotionally neutral concept. It comes preloaded with a lot of baggage. Some people see forgiveness as impossible, or even undesirable, given whom they have to forgive. They simply may not want to or even be able to forgive the individuals involved for the terrible things they have done. Still others may view forgiveness as a religious practice, and because such individuals don't see themselves as religious, they reject it out of hand.

To address these concerns, I have broken forgiveness into three distinct dimensions. They are:

- Relational forgiveness

- Spiritual forgiveness

- Personal forgiveness

Forgiveness involves all three of these dimensions to some degree, yet I find significant advantages in separating forgiveness into these distinct aspects. By doing so we come to understand how it is possible to make progress in one dimension even if we hit a roadblock in another.

Relational forgiveness

Relational forgiveness focuses on what happens between two people when a conflict arises. For relational forgiveness to take place, one person has to ask for forgiveness and the other person has to grant it. In this way, the conflict gets resolved so the two can continue working and living together. Although reconciliation may be the ultimate goal of relational forgiveness, it is not always possible. If one person chooses not to offer forgiveness or the other refuses to accept forgiveness, then relational forgiveness cannot bring about the reconciliation it seeks. Still, real forgiveness can happen without reconciliation. More on that to come.

Spiritual forgiveness

Researchers have found that the word *forgiveness* is most frequently used by people who seek to have their sins forgiven by God—yet you don't need to be religious to see the value of forgiveness or to deal with the hurts you've experienced because of what other people have said and done to you. Those hurts others inflict on you can turn your world completely upside down. The spiritual dimension of forgiveness can help you get things right side up again; it can help you find personal meaning and purpose regardless of where you are on your spiritual journey.

Personal forgiveness

At the personal level, forgiveness facilitates your own healing. You recognize your need to let go of resentment. You realize that your failure to forgive is burning a hole in your soul and ruining your life. You also come to understand that there is no value in holding on to your grudge so, by your act of forgiveness, you let that hurt go. This aspect of forgiveness has the most therapeutic and healing value of the three, for it can help you along your journey from hurt to healing, from victim to victor, and from bitter to better.

So this is the dimension of forgiveness I will focus on in this book. I chose this not only because you have the most control over this type of forgiveness, but also because it offers the greatest immediate benefits for you physically, emotionally, and spiritually. In one sense, personal forgiveness is the starting point for the other dimensions of forgiveness because until you yourself are healthy, you're unlikely to develop healthy relationships with others.

A SKILL TO BE LEARNED

You've probably heard the saying "To err is human; to forgive, divine." While I would agree that to err is human, I would also assert that forgiveness is something we humans can do. In fact, the ability to forgive is the test of our very humanity.

Forgiveness is not some lofty ideal only to be imagined but never reached. Instead, forgiveness is a very effective and practical way of dealing with life's disappointments. Forgiveness is a learned skill that, with practice, you can effectively use. You probably already know that you should forgive. You probably even want to forgive. Maybe you've already tried it . . . but with little success. In this book, I will teach you, step-by-step, *how* to forgive.

When you choose the way of forgiveness, you choose a different path for your life, one that leads toward hope and a better future rather than down a dark path of grievance and pain. Forgiveness means giving up all hope for a better past and instead planning for a better future. Only when you learn to forgive can you experience peace in the present and hope for the future. In short, forgiveness is the work you need to do for your own health and well-being.

This is what I mean by *Forgive to Live.*

Ten Principles of Forgiveness

Forgiveness begins when you . . .

1. Accept that life is not fair and that others may play by a different set of rules than you do.

2. Stop blaming others for your circumstances.

3. Understand that you cannot change the person who hurt you; you can only change yourself.

4. Acknowledge the anger and hurt that some unpleasant or even harmful event is causing you.

5. Reframe your story of hurt—your "grievance story"—by placing the hurtful events in a broader context than your current point of view.

6. Recognize that only you can make the choice to forgive.

7. Shift your view of the offender by humbly choosing to empathize with his or her life situation.

8. Intentionally move from discontent toward contentment.

9. Understand that forgiveness will take time and cannot be rushed.

10. Take responsibility for your life and your future.

If you want to live, at some point you must choose to forgive.

A PARABLE ABOUT FORGIVENESS

DROP THE ROCK!

L ife is hard in Dura . . ."
Countless times each day, that lament was heard from the townspeople—and for good reason. Through the years, Dura had become—literally—a very hard place to live. Rocks covered the landscape, making it impossible to grow flowers or jog in the park. Rocks lay everywhere in the land.

How did this come to be? Well, as the tragic story goes, an evil sorcerer cast a powerful spell upon the town:

> *Through your eyes you will not see*
> *A life of joy or hope or glee.*
> *Through your mouths, where curses flock,*
> *Every angry word shall turn into a rock.*

Whenever someone spoke an unkind or hurtful word, it instantly became a hot rock.

Like everyone in Dura, Kaas had too often been the victim of unkind and hurtful words. Rocks of all sizes and shapes had pelted him. And, also like everyone else in Dura, Kaas never felt content to merely watch those rocks fall to the ground. How could he? They had hurt too much when they struck him!

That's why Kaas developed the habit of keeping a rock or two in his hands. If the occasion presented itself, he could throw one back at the person who had caused him pain. However ugly that strategy might sound, no one ever confronted Kaas about his behavior because everyone in Dura did the very same thing. Oh, they all

11

knew from experience that holding a hot rock would blister their hands, but they believed the pain would be worth it once they got the opportunity—someday—to even the score by throwing back a rock at the one who had hurt them.

When a rock began to cool (as it always did), the people of Dura took it to the center of town where an enormous furnace named Grievance stood. There they could heat up their rock until it once more glowed fiery red, and as it was warming, they told each other their sorrowful tales. "It's not my fault that my hands are burned," each would say. "It's *their* fault. They threw the rock first. I'm just holding it so that someday I can throw it back."

One day, however, Kaas and the other people of Dura got the shock of their lives. A robust, cheerful man with compassion in his eyes came striding into town, declaring that none of the townspeople had to live in misery any longer.

"My name's Sala," he announced, "and I want you to know that you can be free of those rocks you carry around wherever you go. What you need is *forgiveness*. You don't have to keep living like you have been."

Some of the townspeople sneered, while others gasped or stared blankly ahead. *Could there really be a better life? Impossible!*

Sala ignored the jeers and continued. "Simply put, forgiveness is learning how to drop your rocks. You don't have to collect them, carry them, be burdened by them, heat them, or throw them. In fact, I guarantee that, if you drop them, your whole life will improve. Your hands will start to heal. And you'll have the time and the energy to do the fun things you've always wanted to do, but never believed you could."

It can't be that simple, Kaas thought. *How could it possibly work?* He had to speak out.

"Now, hold on, mister," Kaas began. "You mean to tell me that if someone throws a rock at me, I can't throw it back? That's not fair! Why should I let the other guy off the hook? He needs to be punished! No, sir, your way won't work. And I am not falling for it!"

With that, Kaas spun on his heels and hustled away as fast as he could from Sala and his too-good-to-be-true words. In his headlong retreat, however, Kaas failed to notice that a few in the crowd had already decided to give Sala's counsel a try. They dropped their rocks—and immediately noticed something truly remarkable. The scars on their hands, caused by carrying the hot rocks for so many years, began to heal.

These people had always worried that forgiving would be letting their offenders off the hook, but—they learned—dropping their rocks actually made their own lives better. Soon the people of Dura were throwing fewer rocks, so fewer rocks came hurling back at them. In fact, in some yards, the rocks were so scarce that flowers began to break through the newly exposed ground.

Who would have believed that life's burdens could be so easily removed by simply dropping the rock?

ONE

LIFE SHOULD BE FAIR

It's very hard to assure equality . . .
Some men are killed in war, others are wounded,
and some never leave the country.

—John F. Kennedy

L ife isn't fair.

But most of us believe it should be. And why not? It's only fair that life should be fair. Every single one of us wants to think that we're guaranteed a fair shake in life. If I'm a good boy, then good things should happen to me. Yes, life should be fair.

Yet it is exactly this belief that causes us so much heartache and makes forgiveness so hard. Why?

Because even if we think life *should* be fair, it often isn't.

FROM CHILDHOOD ON

We were children when we first learned that life should be fair. We were taught that if we played fairly with others, they would play fairly with us. So I shared my toys with you and expected you to share your toys with me.

In elementary school many of us had this fairness lesson reinforced daily as we repeated the Pledge of Allegiance: "one nation, under God, indivisible, with liberty and justice *for all*." This commitment to universal justice implies that life should be fair. After all, if we are all created equal—as our social studies teachers insisted—then all of us deserve to be treated equally. It's only fair.

So in high school we gave a friend a ride, and we were certain that when we needed a lift, that friend would make a set of wheels available.

In college, we helped a roommate with homework, and we assumed that she would help us when we needed it.

When we got married, we vowed to be faithful, and we were confident that the one we loved would remain faithful to us. And why wouldn't we feel such confidence? After all, fair is fair.

IN THE EYES OF THE BEHOLDER

As a society we place a lot of stock on the golden rule: "Do unto others as you would have them do unto you." And this guideline, if we all lived by it, would indeed guarantee fairness in life. But not all of us live according to this principle, and even those of us who try aren't 100 percent consistent. So, in an effort to be sure that we all play the game of life fairly, society makes rules and passes laws. Without rules, anarchy would reign.

Actually, all relationships are governed by spoken as well as unspoken rules. These rules may range from parental guidance to religious values, from community norms to general life experiences. Whatever their source, these rules govern our expectations of how others should treat us. As long as other people meet our expectations and we meet theirs, our relationships bring mutual satisfaction.

Sounds good—but there's a problem, and it's a big one. The trouble is that *fairness is often in the eyes of the beholder*. After all, each one of us has our own sense of moral justice based upon the cultural or religious values we embrace. Therefore different individuals hold differing (and often conflicting) moral values. At some point those values will clash, and someone will feel the sting of unfairness. In other words, what seems fair to you may seem extremely unfair to me.

Your boss, for example, may think it fair to require you to stay late one night to finish a project. Now, we all know that everyone needs to pitch in with a little extra effort from time to time. Fair's fair. But you may have already promised your wife and kids that you would spend a special evening with them. Besides, you've already put in a lot of overtime on that project. So, to you, your boss's expectation feels very *un*fair.

Another case in point. The law says we must all drive the speed limit and stay in our lane. But if someone cuts in front of me and I have to slam on the brakes and coffee spills in my lap, the other guy hasn't played by the rules—and yet who suffers the consequences? I do. Life is not fair.

Even in our play, rules govern fairness. In sports, competitors have to follow a detailed set of rules. Should players get caught breaking the rules, those individuals are called for a foul, and their team is penalized.

Have you ever played a game where the other person makes up the rules as the game goes along? That's not fun, nor is it fair. And yet many people make up the rules of life as they go. They design rules to suit their own purposes with no regard for how their behaviors may affect someone else. And that's not fair!

Whoever we are, we all expect life to be fair. Physicians want to decide what is best for their patients—but managed care is changing the rules. Homeowners want to know that they can keep their homes for life—but Congress is widening the scope of eminent domain. We want gas prices to remain stable—but big oil raises prices every time it rains. Where's the fairness in any of this?

We want life to be fair so that our lives will remain stable, and we will know how to manage our affairs. Inevitably, though, someone else refuses to live by our set of rules, and a violation occurs. And when we're the ones hurt, we're the ones stuck with the consequences . . . and that *can't* be fair!

WORKING TO RESTORE BALANCE

When someone treats me unfairly, I typically respond with anger. I feel upset, hurt, and frustrated by this violation against me. In fact, I perceive it as a personal attack—probably deliberate and certainly evil.

I begin thinking about the violation, mulling it over, pondering it, brooding over it, stewing over it: *Why did he do that? What was he trying to get from me? What a bad person. Evil. Terrible! I have to do something! He dropped a bomb on me, I have to drop a bomb on him. "An eye for an eye, a tooth for a tooth"—that seems fair to me.* The natural response to being hurt is wanting to even the score: *I have to get back. I was moving along on such an even keel, but now I have to rebalance my life.* That's the reason why, when someone takes from me, I focus my energy on taking back from her. It's my attempt to make things fair.

For many reasons this sense of fairness is a good thing. It gives us the energy and determination to take a stand against injustices. It allows us to live together and get along. And when our attempts to regain fairness work, we do get a real feeling of satisfaction.

Sometimes, however, no matter what you do, you cannot ensure that every situation will be fair. And when you cannot achieve fairness, you naturally respond with hurt and anger and immediately go to work to get back on an even keel. Such efforts usually follow a definite progression.

1. You try to win an apology.

As the wronged party, you attempt to get the other person to admit the offense and, by apologizing, restore some sense of fairness to life. If that happens, then you can go on. Since the violator made up for the wrong, you can move ahead.

But what happens if the other person sees no need to apologize? What if he refuses to make restitution? What if she won't even admit that she offended or hurt you?

2. When the apology doesn't come, you feel additional hurt, and your anger becomes resentment.

If the party who hurt you does not admit the offense and apologize for it, you are left holding a bag that's filling up with more hurt and anger. Suddenly you're facing a truth that shakes your world to its core: *life really **isn't** fair.* Some come to this realization earlier in life than others, but we will all face this situation at some time.

Remember, you were taught as a child that if you play by the rules, everything will work out OK. If you share your toys with others, they will share their toys with you. But *this* person—this wretch, this villain, this lowlife—not only refuses to apologize, but won't even admit that he or she is responsible for your hurt. And that makes you very angry! You are left feeling violated and taken advantage of. And often more than a little resentful.

3. Anger gives you the energy to act.

It is your anger that gives you the energy either to seek some sort of vengeance or to muster support and understanding from others. After all, offenders must be punished. You therefore need to strike back somehow so this person who did you wrong can feel some of the pain that he or she inflicted upon you. Again, your anger gives you the energy you need to attempt to restore fairness in your life.

When you were little, you would tell your mommy about the wrong done to you. She probably would have been understanding and helped you feel better. But, as an adult, who do you turn to? Who will understand you and make things better? Some may hire a lawyer to file suit and seek some kind of financial compensation in court. Or maybe you consider damaging one of the offender's treasured possessions. Maybe you try to ruin his reputation. Maybe you take away something she loves. Whatever you choose to do, you strike back in an attempt to balance the score—in short, to make life fair again.

4. When you don't act, you fantasize about revenge.

But we don't often act on our fantasies. Sometimes we don't act because of our fear of being caught. Sometimes our own moral values prevent us from returning evil for evil. No matter what the reason, we are the ones left holding the bag with no way of evening the score, so our anger often bubbles just beneath the surface as some form of bitterness. You may never admit you're angry, but you do hold a grudge, and you find yourself continually repeating—to yourself or to others—the terrible story of what's happened to you. You turn over in your mind all the possible ways of getting back, of getting even, of balancing the books, of evening the score, and of making life fair once more.

As you contemplate, dwell on, and dissect the awful thing your tormentor did to you, if/then thinking takes over:

- If I send a blistering e-mail, then she will have to apologize.

- If I stop talking to him, then he'll feel so bad that he'll finally make it right.

- If I tell all my friends what she did, then they'll see what a terrible person she is and cut her out of our circle.

Soon such thoughts begin to steal an increasing amount of your time and energy. Your mind, like everyone else's, finds it easy to work overtime on all sorts of if/then scenarios—some of which you might actually try, most of which you would never attempt—but they all have one thing in common: *they almost never work.* The if/then scenarios that bubble and pop and roil in your brain have almost no chance of ever making the situation fair again. Their real effect, in fact, is to keep you chained to an undesirable past and a bleak future.

To make things worse, one retaliatory act of vengeance often spurs a reciprocal response until a cycle of actions and reactions spins out of control. It can become like the infamous feud between the Hatfields and the McCoys. They know they are still fighting, but who can recall exactly what started it all? Such a story cannot possibly have a good ending.

5. *You withdraw from life.*

Few people act out any of the vengeance scenarios they create in their minds. Oh, like many others, you may spend a lot of time brewing up the plans, but either you fear reprisal of some kind (legal, economic, relational), or you simply don't have the heart to carry out your vengeful fantasies. In either case, you eventually begin to withdraw from life.

A feeling of overwhelming helplessness sweeps over you, and you start to move away from the people and activities you once enjoyed. You withdraw like this because you don't want to get hurt in the same way again, or you simply want to avoid the conflict and the person who treated you so unfairly.

Although withdrawal lessens the chance you will be hurt in the same way again, it also guarantees that you will not enjoy life the way you really want to. The more you withdraw, the more isolated you become and the more lonely and diminished you feel. How is that a victory over the person who hurt you?

THE ONLY WAY OUT: FORGIVENESS

Often your attempt to restore fairness will fail. While a certain, temporary pleasure might come from hurting the one who hurt you, in the end it not only leaves a bad taste in your mouth, but it also leaves a bad scar on your soul. So what does work?

Forgiveness.

I have to be kidding, right? Why should you let this person off the hook when he or she deserves to be blamed? That is not fair! Maybe not, but you will see in this book that forgiveness is actually the best thing you can do for yourself.

I want to offer a clear road map that shows how you can find health and wholeness by forgiving the ones who hurt you. *Forgive to Live* isn't just a catchy title or an easy-to-remember slogan. It's actually a concise description of an effective way to function in our unfair world. As you will discover, forgiveness is not the easy road, but it is the better road.

Some of you might think of forgiveness as the obvious answer to life's hurts since forgiveness allows everyone to move on. But here's the catch: forgiveness, at its core, doesn't feel fair. In fact, to forgive forces us to accept something that we don't want to accept: namely, that life *isn't* fair. The act of forgiveness recognizes and even trumpets that life isn't fair.

The truth is, forgiveness does *not* balance the scales of justice any more than vengeance does. But it will keep your past from destroying your future.

Again, forgiveness is difficult because we all want to believe that life is fair. I know I do! Yet letting the other person off the hook seems so *un*fair. That is why many hurting people resist forgiving those who hurt them.

Do you still believe that life is fair? I see nothing wrong with *wanting* it to be fair. Nor is there anything wrong with seeking justice to make things as fair as you can. But, at the end of the day, neither you nor I can control the actions of others. We cannot foresee and prevent every bad thing that happens in life. And since that's indisputably so, it is clearly impossible to make life fair in every situation.

Once you accept this truth, your only viable option is to learn to forgive. Only through forgiveness can you be set free to go on with your life. Join me on this journey as you learn to forgive to live.

A PERSONAL TESTIMONY

I did not reach this conclusion as a result of mere intellectual curiosity. I do not write from an ivory tower. My own experience of undeserved hurt—discovering firsthand that life is not fair despite my demands to the contrary—led me to the place where I could authentically write a book on how to forgive.

For ten years I worked very hard for an organization I deeply believed in. When the company experienced a downturn, it brought in an outside firm to do something called "re-engineering," a fancy name for figuring out ways to cut costs. In a service industry—and that's where I was—the primary cost is labor. So company officials started circling employees' names and handing them the infamous pink slip, stating that their employment with the company had come to an abrupt end.

I got one of those slips.

I felt devastated. How could this be? I had always received stellar performance reviews. My bosses called me a great worker. My co-workers all liked me. The people I reported to were personal friends of mine; we often did things together socially. And yet I went into work one day, was handed a note, and was told curtly, "Today's your last day of work. Pack up and go." And that was it—after I'd been there all those years!

Like anyone else, I went through the stages of grief with the loss of my job. First came shock: I couldn't believe I'd been let go. And then denial: "No, it couldn't be me! There are a lot of other people they should have fired before me. I'm a hard worker. I delivered. I'm well liked. It can't be!" But I couldn't escape the reality that I was not going in to work the next day.

As the truth settled in, I found myself getting increasingly angry and feeling more and more hurt. But I had no idea what to do with all these feelings. What could I do to get my job back? Answer: nothing.

Then I started thinking: *I have to do something! It's not fair! Maybe I can contact someone on the board. Maybe I should go to that person's house and explain how bad this decision was.* I started fantasizing about what I could do to get back, to get even, to balance the score. Even though I never acted on my fantasies, I just couldn't let them go.

Obviously I had to work, so I eventually found another job with a different company. But I soon made some startling discoveries. For one thing, I had a hard time investing in my work. *I'm not going to give any company my all, my 120 percent plus again*, I thought. *Why should I? I'm not going to give my sweat and blood to another organization when people can just fire me tomorrow if they want to.*

I also noticed that I didn't have the energy and passion for my work that I once had. I felt worn out, tired, exhausted. I did the job, but it didn't excite me. I felt deeply discouraged and didn't care much about anything. I certainly wasn't happy.

In time I began putting on weight. My blood pressure shot up. My doctor told me, "We're going to have to put you on a blood-pressure-lowering medication." His words struck me hard. I had always been athletic and had never suffered from any disease, but suddenly I heard from my doctor that I needed to start taking drugs. Something big was going on here!

As I reflected on my current life situation, I discovered that I was holding on to a huge amount of resentment about what had happened in my previous job. I was spending a great deal of energy thinking about my grievance story and what I could do to get back at the people at my former workplace who had hurt me. I felt perfectly justified in thinking those things—but eventually I began to realize the extremely high price I was paying by thinking this way. Even though in my mind I was trying to make *them* pay a price and therefore make life fair, the truth was that, two years after I'd lost my job, the only one paying a price was *me*.

My health suffered in three primary areas:

- *Spiritually*, I was feeling crummy about life and had begun to question whether it had any meaning or purpose. My days seemed to consist of nothing more than waking, working, eating, sleeping, and then starting all over again with exactly the same routine the next day. Was this all there was to being alive? Would this be my day-to-day experience for the rest of my life?

- *Psychologically,* I didn't see myself as angry—I wasn't shouting or screaming or pounding walls—but my wife assured me that my short temper had grown even shorter. I had an edge in my voice whenever she said something that hit me the wrong way. My anger had settled into a deep resentment that revealed itself in my continual recalling of how terribly I had been mistreated. I certainly wasn't relaxed and at peace with life. In fact, I was moving toward depression.

- *Physically,* I was gaining weight, my blood pressure was rising, and I wasn't exercising or even playing anymore. I had no energy, no zest for life, and I felt blah most of the time.

Once I realized what was happening to me and the terrible price I was paying for my reaction to what someone had done to me, I began to read books and articles in an attempt to understand my experience. I also talked to trusted friends. What could I do to let go of this resentment? In time I came across what should have been an obvious answer: forgiveness is a way to let go of unfair situations. Without question, *not* forgiving was saddling me with seriously undesirable consequences. My doctor made it clear that high blood pressure can stem from many factors, but he thought that, in my case, reducing my anger and resentment might provide physical relief.

Now, I had never intended *not* to forgive; in fact, I didn't even realize I had that choice. I was just replaying in my mind the sad story of what had happened to me and my complete inability to do anything about it. But I discovered I wasn't doing *anything* to change my situation for the better—and I was hurting myself.

So I began learning how to forgive. And I can honestly say that it wasn't easy. It didn't happen just by my saying, "OK, I forgive you. Now everything's fine." I had to learn some steps, some processes, some ways of forgiving. Once I began to practice them, my blood pressure gradually returned to normal. I rediscovered a passion for living. I became much less moody at home. And, in learning to let go of my anger, I began to reinvest in life, reenergize my career, and get back on track with my life's purpose.

It felt as though I had discovered a miracle!

My success made me wonder if I could help others learn the same process and enjoy similar benefits. Could I teach people with high blood pressure how to forgive and thereby help them achieve the same results I had? I started teaching about forgiveness, and soon physicians began to refer their patients to me. Eventually I designed a study to investigate whether forgiveness could have measurable health benefits. I took the participants through an eight-week program that taught them the practice and the art of forgiving (see appendix).

The data we collected was nothing short of remarkable. At the beginning of the study, we gave all participants a psychological test that measured anger and hostility. We found that, by the end of the eight weeks, individuals with high blood pressure and elevated anger, who practiced forgiveness as taught in my seminar, were successful at both reducing their anger and lowering their blood pressure. Beyond that, participants spoke a lot about improved relationships and reinvesting in life.

Forgiveness really worked!

So if it worked for me and if it worked for the hundreds of people who came through our "Forgive for Life" training program, I thought I needed to share it with as many people as possible so others might experience for themselves the enormous power of forgiveness.

And that's what this book is about: how to get beyond your anger, move past the undesirable event that's keeping you trapped, and find a healthy solution that will give you back your life. Forgiveness can free you from the past and open the door to a bright world of possibilities that you may not have even dared to imagine.

Forgiveness is not merely a concept to be studied but a practical way to live life. So in each chapter I will invite you to practice what you learn by giving you an assignment. Here's the first one:

ASSIGNMENT

1. What injustice, if any, would you like to correct so life will seem fairer to you? Name that injustice.

2. In the incident you just identified, who hurt you?

3. How has this incident affected you?

4. What attempts to correct this injustice have you made?

5. Take the following test to get a read on your current understanding of forgiveness.

THE FORGIVENESS JOURNEY

Your answers to the following questions will give you a good picture of your current place on the journey toward forgiveness. Be sure to answer each question as honestly as you can.

	YES	NO
1. Do you have a story about someone who has wronged you, someone whom you have yet to forgive?	—	—
2. Are you aware of the price you are paying by not forgiving?	—	—
3. Have you made the choice to forgive?	—	—
4. Are you able to sufficiently change your story of hurt and suffering so it is less painful?	—	—
5. Has your new story of the old event given you a better perspective on life?	—	—
6. When a situation brings you back to feeling helpless, are you able to change that feeling?	—	—

7. Are you making progress toward achieving
   the goals you have set for yourself?   __   __

8. Are you more understanding of the other
   person's circumstances even though you
   disagree with what he or she did?   __   __

9. Have you reconciled with the person involved?   __   __

10. Has forgiveness brought you peace with
    God or greater clarity about your higher
    purpose in life?   __   __

You may not have been able to answer yes to all ten questions, and that should not concern you at this point. You're on a journey of forgiveness. Take one step at a time.

TWO

MY LIFE IS YOUR FAULT

We are taught you must blame your father, your sisters, your brother,
the school, the teacher—but never blame yourself. It's never your fault.
But it's always your fault because if you wanted to change,
you're the one who has got to change.
—Katharine Hepburn

When I was a child, I grew up in the doghouse. I don't mean a literal doghouse, but my parents did have a plaque on the kitchen wall that had five hooks and a doghouse on the end. Any of five dogs—a father, a mother, and three puppies—could be placed on any of the hooks. The collar of each dog sported a nametag—one for each of us. Your dog was hung on the hook in the doghouse if you did something wrong.

I seemed to be a permanent resident.

I also learned early on that, when a problem occurred, the first order of business was to determine who was at fault. In fact, my family tended to put more energy into figuring out whom to blame than in trying to fix the problem.

So, in those childhood days, I never did learn how to apply forgiveness to my troubles. I just continued to live in the doghouse—sometimes for months—until someone else did something bad and chased me out. Because no one let me off the hook—and this time I mean it quite literally—I failed to learn a crucial lesson: *when life isn't fair, we are left with two choices—to blame or to forgive.* I learned how to blame. In fact, most of us find it easier to point the finger than to accept responsibility and figure out what we might need to do in order to solve the problem.

How about you? Have you discovered what you can do to improve your situation, or, like a rusty weather vane stuck in one position, is your finger still pointing toward the ones who have hurt you?

PLAYING THE BLAME GAME

We learn at a very young age to substitute blame for being held accountable for our actions. After all, once we know whom to blame, our problem is solved—or is it?

The Blame Game looks something like this:

1. What happened is your fault.

2. Therefore, the misery in my life is your fault.

In short, my life is your fault. And this way of thinking is a dangerous game that actually solves nothing; it simply assigns blame. If you are playing this game, you need to stop. First of all, blame is like an addiction: it makes you feel better at first, but in the long run it will destroy you. Second, blame never solves a problem. Instead, it merely reinforces your belief that you can do nothing about the situation. At the same time, blame insists that the other person must change before your situation can improve. Blame is really about shifting responsibility so that you don't have to do anything to make things better.

Blame—the idea that "my life is your fault"—keeps your pain raw and throbbing. Blame also drains your energy. Rather than facing your problems and fixing them, you expend more energy than you may realize on fantasizing about ways to get even. Beyond that, blame limits your options. Blame sees only one solution: *the other person must change.* So blame keeps you stuck. Blame also reinforces helplessness. If others need to do something and you can do nothing to change them, then you can do nothing to improve your circumstances. Blame is at the root of your helpless feeling.

In the end, when you blame someone else for your problems, you are in fact saying it is that person's fault and there is nothing you can do about it. Thus, in a very real way, you are giving the other person control over your life. And if you are thinking, *My life is your fault*—no wonder you feel so helpless!

WHY NOT FORGIVE?

If refusing to forgive leaves us holding the bag, then why don't more of us forgive?

Most folks refuse to forgive because they fear that, by doing so, they will let the other person off the hook: "He did me wrong, and if I forgave him, I'd be letting him get away with it. Besides, why should I let him off the hook? That scumbag needs to be punished!" (Does this sound at all familiar to you?) And if you cannot literally dole out the punishment, then at least you can penalize the individual in your mind and, by doing so, create some semblance of justice, right?

Well, not really. In fact, the only one you'll be punishing is yourself.

Remember, no matter what has happened to you, it happened in the past. And the only way you can keep the past alive is in your thoughts. Can you change the past by continuing to think about it? Not in the least. Do you really believe that by *not* forgiving that person, she will change, come to her senses, apologize, and ask for forgiveness? Do you think that somehow your withholding of forgiveness will keep her up at night until she can stand it no longer and comes crawling back to beg for your forgiveness? In one out of ten thousand times that might happen, but it is highly unlikely. And if withholding forgiveness hasn't had the effect you desired over the last year or more, then why would it sometime in the near future? This kind of implausible thinking reminds me of a bumper sticker: "Insanity is doing the same thing over and over again while expecting different results."

So either you can continue to frustrate and hurt yourself by thinking that you can somehow alter what happened by changing the person who offended you, or you can accept what you cannot change. That's the work of forgiveness. It teaches you how to avoid letting the past control your present and insists that you take charge of your thoughts and feelings as they affect you in the here and now. In short, by practicing forgiveness you keep the past in the past and you keep the present, present.

FROM VICTIM TO VICTOR

If you see yourself caught up in the Blame Game, how can you escape? By learning and acting on this simple truth:

"Vengeance hurts me more than it hurts the other person."

Once you understand that truth, you will quickly learn a related one:

"Forgiveness helps me more than it does the other person."

Forgiveness is simply a much better option than vengeance.

The truth is, at one time or another, people *will* treat you unfairly. You cannot avoid being hurt, so you must learn to deal with it. And how can you best do that?

When an injustice is committed against you, you have two choices:

1. Blame the offender and place all the responsibility for improving your life on that person.

2. Forgive, thereby shifting the responsibility to act from the other person to yourself.

Realize that the pathway of blame is nothing more than fool's gold. You think it's worth pursuing, but in the end it brings nothing of lasting value. The pathway of forgiveness may not seem fair at first, but in the end it produces much better results. It is the better choice.

Furthermore, when you blame, you make yourself the victim. By definition, victims are innocent, and abusers are evil. The benefit of being a victim is that you feel innocent. That explains why some people don't want to give up the Blame Game: they fear that either their innocence will be compromised or the guilt of the other will be diminished.

When you forgive the offender, however, you take responsibility for your response to the offense (not for the offense itself); thus you also take responsibility for your life. *Your* actions—not those of someone else—define who you are. You cannot blame others for who you are; your life is your own responsibility. You must choose not to give another person (especially someone you don't even like!) the right to define who you are. While you are not responsible for the hurtful actions of someone else, you are responsible for what you do after someone has wronged you. Your life is your responsibility, and what you do in response to the hurt will determine the person you become.

I define responsibility as your *ability* to choose your *response* to whatever comes your way, thus *response-ability*. Taking action is taking responsibility. And by taking positive action, you move from victim to victor.

What responsibility for your actions are you taking right now? Is your life what you want it to be? If not, are you blaming someone else? If you are playing the Blame Game, then there's nothing you can do to improve your circumstances.

Of course there are real victims in life: an abused child, a person who has been raped, someone who becomes a paraplegic after being struck by a drunk driver. Compassion dictates that we empathize with people in circumstances like these. But even true victims must, at some point, make choices about whether they wish to remain victims or whether they desire to become victors. Some of the greatest heroes I have known are those who overcame the most unimaginable obstacles.

So which do you choose? Forgiveness or blame?

THREE STRATEGIES TO BLUNT BLAME

Later in this book I'll lead you step-by-step on the healing journey of forgiveness, but to give you some relief right now from the powerful urge to blame, let me suggest three strategies that have proven to be very effective.

1. Give up all-or-nothing thinking.

The best way to stop the Blame Game is to move away from all-or-nothing thinking. Learn to see the other person as both good and bad rather than as all bad. Dr. Martin Luther King Jr. reminds us that "there is some good in the worst of us and some evil in the best of us. When we discover this, we are less prone to hate our enemies." So, rather than considering those who have offended you a 100 percent at fault, think of them as 80 percent or 60 percent at fault. When you do this, you are recognizing that *you* also have something—that remaining 20 or 40 percent—to work on. After all, no one is perfect. We all have room for improvement and growth.

You are not to start blaming yourself for what happened, though. That is nothing more than the Blame Game in reverse. Instead, accept that you had at least some part in what happened, even if it was simply making an unwise choice regarding whom to trust. Be willing to face up to the part of the problem you can own; accept your contribution to the situation. You then have the opportunity to learn and grow from every experience in life.

2. Distinguish between intent and impact.

With any offense, you must learn to differentiate *intent* (why those who hurt or offended you did what they did) from *impact* (how those people's actions affected you).

For example, when someone says something critical about your performance, she may have done so to correct a flaw in your behavior so you can do better next time. But if you tell yourself she spoke as she did in order to embarrass you and make herself appear superior to you—you imagine a motive that you cannot verify—then you conclude that the intent of her comment was to humiliate you.

If, however, you consider the impact of the statement—how it hurt you—without trying to assign a motive to it, then you don't make the hurt worse by attributing to the speaker an evil intent that might not exist at all. Besides, how can you ever know for sure the motives behind someone's words or actions? You could base your entire emotional reaction on something you think you know, but which in fact you can never really know. But you do know the impact her comment had on you, and that you can openly discuss. After all, who knows you better than you do?

Now do you see why it is so important to focus on the action (what the person did) rather than on the motive (why the person did it)? If you, however, choose to believe that the individuals who have hurt you acted with the intent of doing evil, the offenses are all the worse, and all-or-nothing thinking is easier to fall into. And that's how you stay trapped in the Blame Game.

3. Lower your expectations of other people.

Your experience of life is due largely to what you expect out of life. If you expect people to act differently than they actually do, then you will often be disappointed and even frustrated. No one in your life will always—at every time and in every circumstance—do what you expect. So to minimize your disappointments, lower your expectations of people. Accepting these two basic truths will help you do just that:

1. People will make mistakes.

2. People do not have to do what you want them to do.

Keep in mind that if you expect support and understanding from someone who doesn't deliver, you are the one who suffers. This is a difficult lesson to learn. We naturally have expectations for one another, especially for those closest to us.

Case in point. Most of us believe that parents should nurture and support their children and that spouses should support each other. Unfortunately, these things do not always happen. And when it's *your* spouse or parents who fall short of your expectations, you are the one left disappointed and perhaps even hurt. The suffering you experience results directly from your expectations. How do I know this? Because a lot of people I don't know give me absolutely no support, yet I don't feel the slightest bit hurt. Why not? Because I don't expect support from total strangers. I'm not saying you shouldn't have expectations of those who are close to you; instead I'm saying to keep those expectations more realistic.

This issue of expectations can feed the often unfounded hope that people who disappoint or annoy you will change. If they have refused to change for the last year, do you really believe that one more appeal from you will convince them to do what you want them to do and meet your needs? If your insistence that they change really could make a difference, those folks would have changed by now. And if they haven't changed yet, the chances of their doing so the next time you ask are very slim.

Forgiveness helps you release or at least revise your expectations.

THE SHORTEST ROUTE TO HAPPINESS

Closely related to the issue of forgiveness is the degree of happiness we experience in life. So consider who is responsible for your happiness. Is it the person who hurt you—or you yourself? The truth is that you are responsible for your own happiness. No one but you. The other truth is that you are more likely to look after your own happiness than someone who doesn't like you.

And the quickest way to happiness is to let go of both your ideas about your "rights" and your sense of what someone else "owes" you. After all, if you have a right to something, you will feel dissatisfied until you have it. As an old proverb puts it, "He who is happy appreciates what he has."

Also, when you believe you have a right to something, you are insisting that someone outside yourself is responsible for ensuring that you get that something. In other words, in order for you to feel life is fair, someone else must provide what you think is rightfully yours. Far too often, of course, people don't meet our expectations or provide for us. What happens then? You're left feeling disappointed, hurt, and frustrated. So what is your alternative? You will find happiness only when you give up your demands that others provide for your needs.

You may want to blame someone else for your unhappiness, but don't give in to that lie. If someone else really were responsible for your happiness, that person would be in charge of your life and have the power to determine your emotional state. And that simply is *not* the way life works.

"Yes, I know I'm responsible for my own happiness," you reply. OK, but do you still think you can't be happy until certain people in your life do something to satisfy you or at least acknowledge that they hurt you? The hard truth is that people may *never* do what you want. So, without realizing it, you may be condemning yourself to a life of unhappiness by looking to others to do for you what only you can do for yourself.

One more thing. The Declaration of Independence does not give you the right to happiness; it merely gives you the right to *pursue* happiness. Only you can make you happy. If you expect someone else to make you happy, you set yourself up for a lifetime of unhappiness.

In the final analysis, happiness is a choice you make. If you choose to be happy, you will be. And forgiveness gives you the power to make that choice. After all, forgiveness releases you from the grip of control over your life that you have given to the offending person. Forgiveness places you back in the driver's seat of your life.

Move Beyond the Pain

Life is like a game of cards. You have no control over what you're dealt, but you have full control over how you play your hand. Forgiveness is a way of playing a bad hand well.

Forgiveness sets you free and allows you to gain wisdom from your suffering as well as to develop strategies for avoiding similar problems in the future. Why would anyone choose revenge at the price of his or her own happiness? So what will you do? Will you continue to blame? Or will you forgive? Remember, forgiveness does not make life fair. But forgiveness does give you back control over your life.

For forgiveness to work, though, you must walk through the pain, not away from it. The Blame Game keeps you stuck exactly where you don't want to be—in the pain. Only by first facing the pain and then forgiving it can you move beyond it.

Assignment

For forgiveness to work, you must identify the person who has caused you pain. Who has hurt you so much that when you think about this person, you feel the hurt all over again? Picture in your mind exactly what that person did to you; recall as many of your feelings as you can. Write out the story of how you were hurt. Then ask yourself these questions:

- Do you think this individual has your best interest at heart?

- If not, why do you give that person so much influence over your happiness?

- Who would you prefer to be responsible for improving your life—you or the person who hurt you?

- Are you willing to take back responsibility for your life *today*?

- Are you willing to forgive this person so you can take back your life and move on?

THREE

FROM BITTER TO BETTER

*Anyone can get angry—that is easy—but to do this to the right person,
to the right extent, at the right time, with the right motive, and in the right way,
that is not for everyone, nor is it easy.*

—Aristotle

Whan I travel across the country doing forgiveness seminars,
I like to ask those in my audience, "If you see yourself as
angry, please raise your hand." Very few people in the crowd, if
any, so much as twitch. Then I ask all those who know someone
who is angry to raise their hands.

Every hand in the house goes up.

It is one of the great mysteries of life: all of us *know* an angry person, but not one of us *is* an angry person.

WHY CAN'T WE SEE IT?

How is it that we can so easily recognize anger in others, but we
rarely see it in ourselves? I think several factors help explain what
goes on.

> 1. *We experience negative emotions four to ten times more intensely
> than we experience positive ones.*

If I were to say five things about you, four positive and one negative, which one are you most likely to think about for the rest of

the day? If you're not sure, try this experiment. Here are five things your best friend just said about you:

- You are a good friend.

- You have been very helpful.

- You tend to tell little white lies.

- You dress very stylishly.

- You were very helpful last night.

Unless you're extremely unusual, you will spend the rest of the day wondering what your friend meant by the "little white lies" you supposedly tell.

"What lies?" you might demand. "If anyone tells lies, it is *you*! Why would you say that about me? I thought you were my friend! I'm going to have to set the record straight and tell all my friends about the white lies you've told."

We all dwell on the negative things said about us; our thoughts and energy naturally gravitate in that direction. If someone gets angry with you and says something negative or does something hurtful, you will remember that event a lot longer than you'd remember something nice that person said or did.

2. We justify our anger.

In those rare moments when we admit that we are angry, we often dredge up some rationale that tries to make our anger seem perfectly understandable, justifiable, and acceptable. We might even think of our emotions as righteous anger, hinting that if the incident had not made us angry, we would not be angry at all. And implied in our defensiveness is that anger comes from without, not from within.

When other people get angry with us, we think they should be able to clearly see how they stepped over the line. Perhaps they have a short fuse, they're constitutionally unpleasant, or they're just plain mean. Or maybe they misunderstood a perfectly innocent comment we made. Whatever the case, their anger is obviously out of control, unjustified, and perhaps even dangerous. Certainly, their anger is nothing like the anger we sometimes exhibit when someone unfairly provokes us. The two reactions are simply not in the same ballpark!

3. We assume the worst possible motives for other people and the best possible motives for ourselves.

When we get angry, we almost always have a perfectly good reason for it. We did not deserve to be hurt. We point out that we responded as gently as any reasonable person possibly could. Or we explain that we had to protect ourselves from serious injury.

But when someone gets angry with us? Well, he's always had it in for us. She didn't even try to understand our point of view. He likes hurting people with his words. She's just plain nasty. We interpret *our* anger and *the other person's* anger in completely different ways.

Here's the snag: whenever two people get angry with each other, both consider themselves the innocent victim and the other the evil abuser. Angry people *always* see themselves as responding justifiably to a wrong, not as initiating that wrong. But I want you to see another reality. Whenever you are angry, you may *feel* like a victim but you *look* like an abuser. And while you are assuming the worst possible motives for your antagonist and the best possible motives for yourself, your antagonist is doing exactly the same thing regarding you.

4. We are trained to believe that showing anger is bad.

If I were to mentally scroll through my personal history, I could describe in detail all the times I've been hurt—but I can barely count on one hand the times I recall being angry. Why is this? I believe it's because, at a very young age, I was taught not to be angry—or at least not to show it.

I distinctly remember an incident from my early childhood

when I got very angry with a friend who provoked me during our playtime. My mother sent me to my room and took away my favorite toy. I learned from that painful incident that getting angry was not an acceptable option, so afterward I tried my best to avoid showing any anger. I feared the rejection and disapproval I had received when I expressed my anger.

In time, I also became frightened of other people's anger. When my parents quarreled, for example, their intensity scared me to death. Hours would go by before I felt safe enough to come out of my hiding place. I feared their anger, and I desperately wanted to avoid it.

How about you? Do you have a hard time admitting when you feel angry? Do you do your best to hide your anger? Do you keep it under lock and key, believing that to express your anger is wrong, dangerous, ugly, and perhaps even unspiritual? Most of us simply cannot admit our anger.

Yet the fact is, we *all* get angry. And a necessary step toward practicing forgiveness is to recognize that you have been hurt and that, as a result, you feel angry.

WHAT IS ANGER?

I define *anger* as "a strong emotion of displeasure brought on by feelings of helplessness and hopelessness." Anger is a response to pain, a wake-up call that something is wrong. You get angry when someone takes away a valuable thing that you believe you can't replace.

The problem is that we have not learned to recognize our anger before it explodes. Anger is not always what it appears to be. The most obvious form of anger is an outburst of shouting accompanied by stinging accusations and heaping bushels of blame. It might surprise you to learn that this is not the most common manifestation of anger. Actually, *resentment* is the most common form of anger—and this covert anger that hides below the surface damages our health more than any of its red-faced cousins.

Because the emotion we call anger burns at various temperatures, you may not recognize something as anger if it doesn't make your veins pop out of your neck. So let's take a look at the continuum of anger.

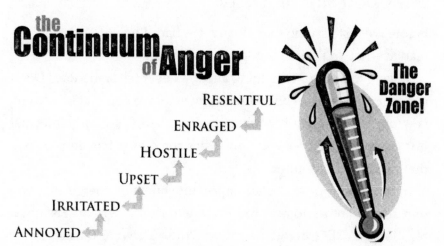

the Continuum of Anger

RESENTFUL
ENRAGED
HOSTILE
UPSET
IRRITATED
ANNOYED

The Danger Zone!

At any point on the continuum, you really are angry even though you may not give your emotions that name. The only difference among these many stages of anger is intensity.

ANGER: A SECONDARY EMOTION

A very fine line separates hurt from anger. Most people do not consider *hurt* and *anger* as even related, but they are, in fact, two different words describing the same thing. Hurt and anger are simply two sides of the same coin.

I become angry when someone hurts me. I may not recognize my anger, but it is always closely connected to the hurt I suffered. Our anger is a reactive emotion, a secondary response, resulting from the primary experience of hurt.

Behavioral psychologists believe that we act as we do largely in response to an outside stimulus. A dog salivates not because it chooses to, for example, but because it smells food. So the behaviorists theorize that human beings, acting in much the same way, get angry not because they choose to but because of the hurt they experience when someone does some awful thing. But I see it differently, as you will soon realize.

THE GOOD SIDE OF ANGER

Before we just assume that all anger is bad, I want to ask you, the reader, what you think: is anger good or bad?

When I talk about managing anger, I never tell someone, "Don't get angry." Anger can be an important signal to you that something is wrong. Anger itself is neither good nor bad; it's simply information. Anger should let you know that something has gone wrong that needs your attention.

In fact, anger provides an important source of energy that you may need in order to act productively to right a wrong. The organization MADD (Mothers Against Drunk Drivers) illustrates the useful and necessary role of anger. After a number of children were needlessly killed in auto accidents caused by intoxicated drivers, the deep *hurt* felt by the mothers over the unnecessary loss of life expressed itself in *anger* against a deadly social situation. That anger provided the necessary motivation and *energy* to create a nationwide organization that has saved countless lives.

Without question, anger serves a useful and even necessary purpose. Consider a few of the clear benefits of anger.

1. Anger indicates that something is wrong.

Think of that first surge of anger as a warning light flashing on and off on the dashboard of your consciousness. It's trying to tell you that something has gone amiss. You don't get angry for no reason at all. You don't get angry because you like to get angry. You get angry when you feel hurt by a loss or an injury of some kind. Your anger tips you off that someone—even if you can't immediately identify who—has in some way committed a violation against you.

2. Anger confronts the concern.

Anger gives you the energy to meet head-on something that you might otherwise choose to avoid. It provides the motivation and the determination to tackle an unpleasant situation that must be addressed. Fear might make cowards of us all, but anger can make us bold.

3. Anger seeks clarification of both goals and barriers.

Hurt may often cloud your vision, but anger can prompt you to determine where you want to be and identify what may be keeping you from getting there. Anger can energize your quest for understanding and keep you moving forward. It helps you both overcome the lethargy often associated with pain and find the answers you need to secure a productive future.

4. Anger prompts you to assert yourself.

There is nothing particularly humble about silently allowing someone to wrongly inflict injury on you. Don't forget that the same religious leader who instructed his followers to "turn the other cheek" also turned over the tables of the moneychangers who were cheating the people.

5. Anger can fuel our efforts to find a winning solution.

If you did not respond to life's hurts with anger, you might never seek out answers to the painful problems you face. I recall several occasions when my anger gave me the energy to assert myself. While I may not have expressed my sentiment with raging anger, it was anger that fueled my passion to speak up.

6. Anger leads to a spirited and rewarding life.

Did you know that the root of the Hebrew word for anger describes the snorting breath of a bull? Anger is energy waiting to act. So don't just blow off steam. Instead work on expressing your anger in a way that identifies the issues and effectively addresses them. Such constructive expressions of anger can actually give you a satisfying sense of accomplishment and renewed energy. When we wisely channel the energy of our anger, we can lead a spirited and rewarding life.

Human anger serves a good and crucial purpose, yet it can much too easily overstay its welcome. The problem is not your anger, but your tendency to get angry more than is necessary and to stay angry longer than is helpful. Getting angry is less of a problem than remaining angry. This reality points to the fact that there is a dark side to anger that can harm us and those around us.

THE BAD SIDE OF ANGER

Some anger is necessary and good, but anger—especially long-held anger that rots into resentment and bitterness—can also be destructive. Such anger can do terrific amounts of damage to both your body and your soul. But if that's true, why do so many people hold on to their bitterness?

Often they believe holding on to their anger is good for them. They mistakenly believe that their resentment provides specific benefits. Consider four very common false benefits of anger cited by habitually angry people:

1. I have someone else to blame for my misery.

We've already looked at the Blame Game, perhaps the most popular false benefit of all. The thinking goes like this: "I'm miserable, and it's all the work of my persecutors. It's not my fault." So, hoping to cause my adversaries some discomfort, I divert all my attention away from myself and onto them.

But consider the wisdom of the late comedian Buddy Hackett. "I've had a few arguments with people, but I never carry a grudge," he said. "You know why? While you're carrying a grudge, they're out dancing."

2. Being a victim means I have less responsibility for my circumstances.

People hang on to their anger, not merely because they want to focus blame on someone else, but because they don't want to be responsible for their own misery. (Yes, this second false benefit is closely tied to the first.) After all, if they're not responsible for their wretched situation, then they don't have to do a thing to change it. In fact, in their mind, there's nothing they *can* do. They're completely at the mercy of someone else. That is why they are angry.

But what kind of a benefit is it to these victims that allows their offenders to keep on hurting them for months, years, even decades after the offense? Not that the victims are literally hurting their offenders, but in their minds the victims are hurting themselves over and over again with every recall of the painful event. In what way does such a "benefit" help the injured ones improve their life? At some point you must ask yourself these two important questions:

- What is it costing me to hold on to my anger?

- Will remaining angry make any significant improvement in my circumstances?

If you have come to the conclusion that it is not in your best interest to hold on to your anger, then it may be time to let go of your anger by forgiving the other person. It may be time to move on.

3. I get attention when I get angry.

Some victims revel in their anger because it gives them a stage, a platform, a podium. If they don't get red-faced, loud, and abusive, no one pays any attention to their stories of ill treatment. Getting an audience may not make them feel much better, but at least they're not suffering alone *and* being ignored. These angry folks are proud poster children for the maxim "Misery loves company." (It rarely occurs to them, however, that their unsuspecting company does *not* love such misery—and so ceases to be company at the earliest possible opportunity to get away.)

4. I feel powerful because I can either intimidate others or manipulate them by making them feel guilty.

Some people use their anger about being hurt to browbeat others into complying with their demands. They bluster and threaten and heap on the pressure until they get their way. Or they use guilt to manipulate others into doing what they want. Using guilt may not look like anger, but it comes from the same well.

While these four reasons for holding on to anger may seem like benefits to those who live by them, clinging to one's anger brings on several inevitable and distressing side effects. Oh, it's true that anger can indeed be a way of asserting your rights—but is your need to even the score so strong that you are willing to give up your need to be happy? That's the unfortunate trade-off: Habitually angry people commonly suffer from overpowering feelings of helplessness, despair, disappointment, sadness, insecurity, and fear. They also become superficial and shallow in their relationships rather than authentic. Is that really what you want for yourself?

In addition, we now know that people who hang on to their anger suffer many serious health problems. In the next chapter we'll take a closer look at the terrible physical repercussions of refusing to let go of anger and resentment. Right now, suffice it to say, your anger can—quite literally—kill you.

Remember the parable at the beginning of this book? Holding on to anger is a lot like holding on to a hot rock. As you clench it tightly in your fist, ready to hurl it at the person who did that awful thing to you, you are in fact hurting only yourself.

THE SEVEN DEADLY STRATEGIES

Most of us not only cling to a few misguided reasons for holding on to our anger, but we also employ several faulty strategies for dealing with anger. Despite their widespread acceptance and practice, not one of the following seven approaches works.

1. *Overlooking the hurt by pretending it didn't happen or by discounting its impact*

"It was nothing." "Forget it. I've had worse things said/done to me." "I've already forgotten that, so let's just get back to business." With statements like these, we deny our hurt and downplay the seriousness of the injury. . . and that kind of unresolved hurt has a nasty tendency to come back and bite us. The relationship with the person who hurt us will also suffer.

2. *Focusing on the unfair behavior of the other person*

It's always easier to see a problem in someone else than it is to see problems in ourselves. But until you can see both sides of the problem, you can't see the real problem. And remember that people who refuse to stop focusing on the hurtful behavior of others— who will not take responsibility for their own happiness—end up discouraged, unhappy, and usually alone.

3. *Displacing anger on a third person*

Some hurt and angry people who can't deal directly with the one who offended them—maybe that person has died, moved away, or is too intimidating—instead focus their anger on a substitute. This substitute is often weaker and therefore more likely to accept the displaced anger without expressing much (if any) objection. While such an arrangement may give one some small, skewed sense of relief, it does nothing to alleviate the serious consequences of their internal bitterness—and in fact creates additional victims with their own hurts and anger.

4. *Denying the anger*

We've already mentioned this one, but it bears repeating. Some of us try to deal with our anger by totally denying that we are angry. Case in point: A counselor friend recently told me about a client who came in to find some relief for his depression. As this man described a succession of unfair events over the years, going back almost two decades, he was spouting profanities, his face turned crimson, and the veins on his neck bulged out alarmingly. When he had finished, my friend asked him what he thought made him so angry. The client looked confused and said, "Angry? I'm not angry."

5. Developing a mental picture of revenge

If we are unable to get an apology or even an admission of guilt from the one who hurt us, we often try to even the score by imagining all sorts of things we could do to exact our revenge and thereby balance the books. These flights of fancy might veer into the world of the highly improbable, or they might seem quite feasible. Whether or not we ever attempt a real-world deed of vengeance, these imaginative thoughts of revenge somehow fool us into believing we are punishing the offender and thus bringing a semblance of fairness back to our inner world—but they never make real life fair.

6. Using drugs, alcohol, or food to numb the pain

Many hurting people don't know how to deal with their anger and can't get rid of the pain, so they try to either drown their dark emotions in a flood of chemicals or smother them under a mountain of groceries. This way of coping may offer some temporary relief, but in the end it only makes a person's problems worse by piling a truckload of medical problems on top of the ones caused more directly by the unresolved anger.

7. Becoming cynical about life

Some of the worst cynics you'll ever meet are angry people who have never effectively dealt with a deep and perhaps long-held hurt. They are able to cleverly mock anything that holds out the promise of a better life. They have become experts in scorn, ridicule, and derision. Since life has not worked out for them the way they once envisioned, they shield themselves by becoming what they call "a realist." They get whatever joy they can from skewering the naive hopes of the gullible.

These seven deadly strategies not only don't work, but they leave people in worse shape than they were initially. If you don't face your anger and employ healthy strategies to effectively handle it, you run the risk of turning your anger into bitterness . . . and that will end up destroying you. So what can you do to begin to deal with your anger in a healthy, productive way?

THREE WAYS TO EXPRESS ANGER

So how do you release your anger so that it doesn't destroy you or those around you? Many of us don't realize that we can decide how to respond to life's hurts, so let me clearly state that all of us really do have the opportunity to choose what to do with our anger. And the choice we make on this issue goes a long way in determining whether we become bitter or better people.

People who have been hurt can express their anger in one of three distinct ways:

- *Passively*—as revealed by such behaviors as ignoring, wishing, withdrawing, accommodating, and avoiding

- *Aggressively*—as revealed by such behaviors as attacking, forcing, criticizing, controlling, and harming others

- *Assertively*—as revealed by such behaviors as confronting, being honest, stating expectations, setting boundaries, and detaching

Passivity waits for the other person to change because it sees no other pathway to improvement. But when you remain passive, you take no responsibility for bringing about a healthier situation. Instead you sit back and hand over the reins of your life to the individual who hurt you. You may do so out of the false belief that you're exhibiting humility, patience, or tolerance. But passivity serves only to gradually transform your anger into bitterness and resentment.

Aggression strikes out in a hostile and even brutal way in an effort to intimidate other people into submission. Every time you aggressively express your anger, you are acting like a bully—and bullies are not powerful. They are weak individuals trying to use their meanness to cover their fears—and the greater their insecurities, the meaner these bullies will be. The only way bullies can feel good about themselves is to see someone else as weaker.

Assertiveness insists on being treated with dignity and respect—and is careful to treat others that way too. When you respond in an assertive way to the one who hurt and angered you, you make clear that you will not accept the mistreatment, but you do so in a manner that affirms both your worth and the other person's.

So, to express and process your anger most effectively, choose the assertive option, not the passive or aggressive path. Assertiveness takes responsibility not necessarily for what happened, but for what will happen now and in the future. What does such a healthy, assertive expression of anger look like? These guidelines will show you.

1. Confront the problem when it arises and face the situation head-on before anger has a chance to fester.

2. State as objectively as you can your point of view and be careful to use "I" statements rather than "you" statements. Say, for example, "I feel like I am not important to you when you come home late without letting me know" instead of "You don't care one bit about me, or you would have called." "I" statements talk about what I need, not about what you must do for me.

3. Make your communication clear and specific. Say, for instance, "It would be helpful if you would call as soon as you know you are going to be late so I can change plans on this end" rather than "What do you think—the whole world revolves around your schedule?"

4. Assertiveness focuses more on the ways you have been hurt than on how angry you are. This can be helpful because other people can listen much more easily to words that express hurt than to words that express anger. Also, assertiveness seeks to clarify and resolve the problem, not to escalate it.

5. Being assertive means setting clear boundaries. If you say no, then mean it. Don't give in for the sake of peace when you know you will regret it afterwards.

6. Establish consequences when necessary, and this will reinforce that you mean what you say.

None of us chooses to become angry, but we most certainly choose how we respond to the hurt that triggered our anger. And if we allow our anger to hang around without effectively dealing with it, then at some level we are choosing to remain angry.

At the end of this chapter, you will find a short and easy test to help you determine the degree of anger you may be harboring. (I recommend that you take the test after you finish reading this chapter, but if you prefer, you may go there now and finish reading after you calculate your results.)

BITTER OR BETTER?

All of us select our path in life by choosing how we respond to life's hurts. Two primary pathways exist, as described on the next page. How you choose to deal with your anger will put you on either the road to bitter or the road to better.

Bitter	**Better**
You make me angry.	I make myself angry.

Therefore

Your actions caused my feelings and behaviors.	My thoughts and actions determine how I feel and what I do.

Therefore

You must change so I can feel better again.	I choose how I live my life.

Therefore

If you do not change, I will resent you, and I will be miserable for the rest of my life.	I am free to do what I need to do for my well-being. I will go on with my life and live happily ever after.

Do you want to move from bitter to better? Bitterness will blind you to what is good in life; it will allow you to see only what is wrong in the world. And eventually bitterness will destroy you.

When you choose to take control of your anger, it will cease to control you. And control in and of itself reduces your anger. Psychologist Marshall Rosenberg expressed it this way: "At the core of all anger is a need that is not being fulfilled." Learn to fill your needs in healthy ways. You will enjoy a longer and more fulfilling.

HOW WILL YOU RESPOND TO LIFE'S HURTS?

None of us lives in a vacuum. We all live in relationships with other people. In those relationships, we sometimes get hurt—and when we get hurt, we get angry.

The question is not how to avoid anger, but what you will do when you get angry. Will you respond passively, a choice that almost guarantees that your anger will morph into a deep and destructive resentment? Will you respond aggressively, practically ensuring that you will both deepen the hurts and begin your own brisk march toward bitterness? Or will you respond assertively, refusing to ignore your hurt even as you take care to treat those who hurt you with dignity and respect?

Often when you're feeling angry, forgiveness is the last thing you think about. And if your anger persists, you will find it harder to forgive because your anger turns into resentment. Choosing the right method of dealing with your anger sets the stage for forgiveness to do its restorative work. Forgiveness breaks the cycle of anger, resentment, and victimization. Forgiveness is the way to work *through* your problems rather than to walk *around* them. Forgiveness heals the hurt rather than hiding it.

One more point here: Hatred that grows from anger can never put an end to hatred; only forgiveness can do that. But forgiveness, as powerful as it is, can work in your life only after you have understood your anger and chosen to deal with it honestly.

Have you?

ASSIGNMENT

Ask yourself the following questions:

1. What will you lose if you let go of your anger?

2. What do you think you will gain by holding on to your anger?

3. In which of the three ways—passively, aggressively, or assertively —do you most frequently express your anger?

4. In which of these three ways would you like to be able to express your anger? Explain why.

5. What would your life be like without your anger?

Now take the anger test that follows and discover whether anger may be a serious problem for you.

ANGER TEST

1. When you go through an express checkout lane in a grocery store, you:
   a. Count the number of items in the carts in front of you
   b. Think about what you will have for supper

2. When you're driving and someone pulls right in front of you, nearly forcing you off the road, you:
   a. Get on the horn and give that #*@%# driver a piece of your mind
   b. Are thankful that you gave yourself enough time so that you do not have to drive like that person

3. When you accidentally stub your big toe, you:
   a. Kick the object with your other good foot
   b. Remind yourself to pay more attention to where you are walking

4. When you see people you don't like, you:
   a. Think of all the bad things each of them has done to you
   b. Remind yourself that they have their own struggles

5. You are more inclined to think about:
   a. People who have hurt you
   b. People who have helped you

6. When waiting for an elevator, you:
   a. Count how long it waits on each floor and wish people would hurry
   b. Talk to the person next to you until the elevator arrives

7. When you make a bad shot on the fairway, you:
   a. Throw your club down on the ground
   b. Analyze your swing to correct any errors

8. When someone doesn't arrive on time, you:
   a. Think of how inconsiderate that person was to keep you waiting
   b. Hope nothing bad happened to cause the delay

9. When somebody makes a joke at your expense, you:
   a. Fire back a put-down of your own
   b. Laugh at the humor

10. When you see a scratch on the side of your car, you:
    a. Scratch the car next to you
    b. Stop by a store to purchase touch-up paint

11. When you get angry, you:
    a. Throw things
    b. Talk about it

12. You most often see your parents as:
    a. Dysfunctional
    b. Human

Now count the number of *a*'s you marked. Here's what the results indicate:

- If you marked three or fewer *a*'s, you do well with your anger.

- If you marked no *a*'s, you may be in denial about your true feelings.

- If you marked between four and seven *a*'s, be aware that you will have difficulties with anger on occasion and you should pay careful attention to your moods.

- If you marked eight or more *a*'s, you have a problem with anger.

FOUR

WHAT YOU TELL
YOURSELF CAN KILL YOU

A merry heart does good like a medicine.

—King Solomon

One day my wife and I visited an amusement park. I enjoy a
good roller-coaster ride, and in the past my daughter and I
always looked for the biggest and baddest coaster we could find.
But my daughter had grown up and left home, so on this particular afternoon, it was just my wife and me at the amusement
park.

And did I tell you that my better half has a morbid fear of roller
coasters? Not because she has ever ridden one; she just fears her
mental image of what a roller-coaster ride might be like.

So when I asked if she would ride with me, she said no. I didn't
want to ride alone, so I used all my training in psychology to convince her that she had been living a deprived existence due to her
failure to ride a roller coaster. At the very least, I suggested, a trau-
matic event from her past must lie at the root of her fear, which she
had transferred to roller coasters. But nothing worked.

So I went back to the basic psychology I'd learned in kinder-
garten: I begged. I promised that if she would ride with me just one
time, I would never ask again. And besides, since she had never

tried it, how could she know she wouldn't like it? After I begged for hours, she finally agreed to join me for just one ride.

Now, if you had just one ride for the day, would you—out of consideration for your wife—choose a beginner roller coaster, or would you go for it and pick the biggest, fastest one in the park? Loving husband that I am, I chose the highest coaster, the one with the most loops, a death-defying monster that dangles your feet in midair.

As we stood in line, anyone around us could see my wife's body change. She tensed up, her heart raced, she grasped my hand so hard it hurt, and the veins in her neck almost burst. In fact, had I taken her to an emergency room, doctors would have immediately admitted her, for she had all the symptoms of an impending heart attack.

We were, however, still standing on the ground, walking at the rate of one step a minute. My wife had nothing to fear while we were inching our way through the line, so why did her body react so strongly? Simple. Because, in her mind, she was already on that horrid coaster. After the ride was over, Arta admitted, "It wasn't as bad as I thought it would be—but I'll never ride another one again!" And she hasn't.

That day I learned that the anticipation of an event can be just as real—in fact, often more real—to the body as the event itself. I saw living proof that one's perspective of reality—rather than reality itself—determines how the body will react.

THE MIND/BODY CONNECTION

Have you ever awakened from a bad dream and found yourself in a sweat with your heart beating rapidly? Perhaps a bear was chasing you. But, in reality, what just happened? Nothing. You were fast asleep, and no bear roamed your room.

That truth doesn't matter to your body, though, because your mind saw the bear as if it were actually there and signaled your body to react accordingly. Your heart rate shot up, and the fuel burning in your muscles produced heat, causing you to break out in a sweat.

This mind/body connection is obvious in more than just our responses to a harrowing dream. For instance, statistics inform us that heart attacks occur on one day of the week more than on any other—and even at a particular time of that day. Can you guess when? If you said Monday morning, you were right. Vast numbers of people don't enjoy their jobs, and the mere thought of returning to work can stress a weakened heart and contribute to a fatal heart attack. The mind/body connection is very powerful!

EXPERIENCE THE PHENOMENON

I'd like you to experience this mind/body interaction right now. The instructions are simple. Just squeeze your fist as hard as you can for five seconds. Ready? Begin squeezing—5 . . . 4 . . . 3 . . . 2 . . . 1 . . . stop.

What was happening in your body during those five seconds? You probably noticed that you clenched your jaw and tightened the muscles up your arm and even into your back. Did you notice that you held your breath? (You did! Who told you to do that?) You also slowed your digestion, released certain hormones into your bloodstream, increased your heart rate and blood pressure, altered your cholesterol levels, and even suppressed your immune system. You didn't know you were doing all these things, but that is precisely what your mind directed your body to do—all below your level of awareness.

Now repeat the experiment. Once again squeeze your fist as hard as you can, but now laugh at the same time. Ready? Begin squeezing and laughing—5 . . . 4 . . . 3 . . . 2 . . . 1 . . . stop.

Did you notice anything different happening in your body this time? You didn't squeeze as hard, did you? And there was less tension in your body. You breathed, your body released different hormones, your heart rate and blood pressure did not increase as much, and your immune system may actually have benefited from the exercise. Even though you were using the same muscles in both experiments, you could not squeeze as hard while you were laughing. Even elite athletes, given squeeze meters that measure force in pounds per square inch, cannot squeeze as hard while they're laughing.

Why these different results? Because the brain's message to the body was not clear. Your laughter confused your mind, and it wasn't sure whether to feel anger or happiness. So your mind couldn't send a clear message to your body. That's why, in the second experiment, your body reacted differently even though you consciously gave it the same message to squeeze as hard as you can and you used the same muscles.

ANGER KILLS

What you think in your mind has a profound impact on what happens in your body. This is especially true when your thoughts focus on angry or hostile feelings. Researchers have found that prolonged anger has a devastating effect on physical health.

In numerous studies, Dr. Redford Williams at Duke University clearly demonstrated that anger kills. In one study, for instance, he reviewed the anger scores of 225 physicians who had graduated twenty-five years earlier from medical school at the University of North Carolina. When they first began their medical training, each student was required to take a psychological test, part of which measured hostility or anger. Dr. Williams arranged the old anger scores from the highest to the lowest. Then he sent out a questionnaire asking these physicians about their current health.

Dr. Williams discovered that those people with the highest anger scores while they were in medical school also had the highest incidences of heart disease and death twenty-five years later. He used this data to support his theory that a person's anger can actually predict illness, particularly heart disease.

The science behind this study was so convincing that the American Heart Association declared anger a risk factor for heart disease, right alongside other standard markers like cholesterol, exercise, and nutrition. The May 5, 2000, issue of *Circulation* warned, "A person who is most prone to anger is three times more likely to have a heart attack than someone who is least prone to anger."

Recent studies have also shown a link between sustained anger and headaches, stomach disorders, joint pain, fatigue, and chronic lower back pain. This last problem happens in part because your muscles are wrapped into your spinal cord, the point from which your nerves stimulate and move the muscles, and because the last of the muscles to relax are those closest to the spine.

Again, the point should be clear: anger kills.

ACUTE VS. CHRONIC STRESSORS

I need to make an important distinction between acute and chronic stress. Acute stress occurs when a threatening event appears and then is quickly resolved. Your body is well designed to handle acute stress; in fact, your body can even benefit from stress. Much in the same way that exercise works, acute stress can help you become stronger so you're better prepared physically for future emergencies.

On the other hand, chronic stress—when the event remains constantly on your mind and does not go away—can harm you. Why? Because your body has no recovery phase during which to rest and rebuild. That lack of downtime both depletes your body's reserves and postpones long-term rebuilding, which causes the premature deterioration of major organ systems. Serious illness and even death may result.

Again, the difference in duration between acute and chronic stress is key. Elevated blood pressure is fine when you face an immediate danger (acute stress). If a grizzly bear really is chasing you, you want an immediate surge of energy in order to escape the slashing claws and glistening teeth. But if you constantly worry that a bear may be stalking you (chronic stress), you will always maintain an elevated blood pressure—and a constant blood pressure of 180/120 will kill you more surely than any bear attack.

The real culprit is not your body's initial response to stress. That initial response—the increased heart rate, increased blood pressure, change of kidney function, release of fat into the bloodstream, and increased cholesterol in your bloodstream—is not the problem. The problem comes when these systems are left turned on for prolonged periods of time. That is when your health is at risk.

THE PROBLEM OF REPRESSION

"Whew, I'm out of the woods," you say. "I'm not chronically angry with anyone, so I shouldn't have to worry about bears or heart attacks or strokes."

I hope that's true, but you need to know that the brain works in a lot of funny ways. For example, it tends to repress certain things. Whatever you—and the rest of us—find unpleasant, you tend to repress rather than deal with and move on. Instead of thinking about a troubling thought or experiencing a negative feeling, you push it out of your mind so you are no longer aware of it. But repression does not make the problem go away or reverse its negative effect on your body. Repression simply moves the idea or emotion from your conscious to your unconscious level of thinking.

Repression can occur intentionally or unintentionally. You may say to yourself, "I don't want to deal with that situation now," so you push your feelings to the back of your mind and move on. In that case, you intentionally repress those emotions you don't want to feel. Usually, however, repression occurs outside of your awareness. Your past experiences may have shaped your habit of avoiding certain feelings (by repressing them) even before you become aware of their presence. Of course you're more likely to repress negative feelings (who would want to repress enjoyable feelings?), and those negative feelings are the ones most likely to damage your health.

This process of repression is especially significant when it comes to dealing with anger. People who hold on to anger are the most stressed individuals that doctors see, and these people suffer the most physical ailments, such as headaches, stomach problems, muscle tension, and high blood pressure.

One more note on the physical effects of anger. Would it surprise you to learn that, by drawing your blood and reading its chemical composition, specialists in the lab can literally measure your emotions? Scientists can accurately read your feelings by doing a chemical analysis of your blood: your anger, for example, releases a chemical messenger called cortisol that acts on many of the major organ systems of your body. The physical effects of your anger are very real.

But habitually angry people also suffer emotionally. Their broken lives are full of bitterness, resentment, hurt, and anger. They interpret everything that happens through those dark lenses. When someone does something hurtful, they immediately think, *That person's out to get me.* If the incident remotely resembles some past offense, they say, "It's the same rotten thing all over again." These people live in their world of bitterness and resentment, and they're convinced that others have forced them to live there. Seldom do they realize that they themselves have chosen to inhabit that world of pain.

Finally, chronically angry people suffer spiritually. They lack a real sense of purpose and have a hard time investing in life. Because life has been so unfair to them, they fail to fully experience the beauty and excitement and adventure and joy that life has to offer. Their perception of reality makes them angry, and—as we've seen—anger is a primary contributor to the chronic stress that, in turn, affects their health. It's no surprise, then, that chronically angry people too often pay for their anger with their life.

THE HEALING PROPERTIES OF YOUR MIND

Think for a moment about that no-good snake in the grass who did you harm. Every time you see or even think about that person, you experience your anger anew.

But if you interpreted the situation differently, would you react in the same way? Probably not because it is your interpretation of the hurtful event that triggers your anger. If you can learn to see the person differently by reshaping your memory of the event, your body will react in a completely different manner. In fact, some people out there don't see this individual as a snake in the grass at all but rather as a friend. Different people will have different perceptions of the same reality.

Remember, it is not reality but your perception of reality that affects your body. And that is good news because while you cannot change reality, you can change your perceptions.

Let's take this notion that reality is rooted in our perspective one step further. Suppose two people see a snake. One person jumps back and screams in terror, but the other reaches out in delight to pick up the slithering creature. They both see the same snake. The different reactions are due to their different interpretations; the snake doesn't mean the same to both of them. As Carl Jung once said, "It all depends on how we look at things, and not on how things are in themselves."

The drawings below illustrate this principle. Look at drawing

DRAWING 1   DRAWING 2

number one. What do you see? Now look at drawing number two. What do you see there?

Most people see a young princess in the first drawing and an old woman in the second. But these are *exactly the same pictures*. One is simply turned upside down. Your perspective really does determine your reality, and you really can use your mind to change your perspective. By doing so, you can keep your anger from destroying your life. So let your thoughts heal you rather than kill you!

The Placebo Effect

The medical community has known for years that the mind can foster the body's healing. It's called the placebo effect. In fact, a placebo—nothing more than a sugar pill—is used in most clinical trials of new drugs. The Federal Drug Administration will approve only those drugs proven to be more effective than a placebo.

Participants in these clinical trials are not told if they are taking a sugar pill or the real medicine, but most believe they are getting real medicine. Despite signing a consent form that explains the study and its design, the participants expect to get real medicine for their real illness. Do you know that some people who get nothing but a placebo actually show physical improvement in their very real medical conditions?

What makes this little sugar pill so effective? Nothing but the power of the mind. The placebo did nothing chemically for the body, but it did set up the expectation in your mind that something good will happen. If you think you are taking a pill that will help you heal, your body will react as though you really had. Forgiveness takes advantage of these mind-body interactions to heal the devastating effects of prolonged anger.

Let Forgiveness Heal You

Unresolved anger can lead directly to heart disease and other serious illnesses, but by practicing forgiveness you can reverse its harmful effects. Researcher Fred Luskin used standardized anger expression tests to measure scientifically the beneficial reductions in anger one can achieve by practicing forgiveness.

In another study, Charlotte Witvliet simply asked people to imagine someone from the past who had caused them harm. As they did so, their bodies reacted with increased blood pressure, a higher heart rate, sweaty palms, and muscle tension in their forehead. Dr. Witvliet then asked participants to imagine what it would be like to forgive the individual they had imagined. She did not teach anyone how to forgive; she merely asked them to think of the *possibility* of forgiving. When they did this, all the physiological measures mentioned above reversed. Forgiveness directly affected physiology.

The clinical study I did investigating the relationship between forgiveness and blood pressure (see appendix) taught me that people who learn to practice forgiveness:

- Believe they can do something about their condition

- Move the locus of control from what someone else did to what they need to do

- Begin the process of letting go, changing their grievance stories, and moving on with their lives

- Were able to significantly lower their blood pressure

During interviews at the end of each forgiveness training program, I invited participants to describe what they found most helpful in our weeks together. Each time I expected them to say something like "I feel good about being able to reduce my anger" or "I was delighted to lower my blood pressure"—answers that would reflect the two major emphases of the program. But you know what I heard most often? It may surprise you.

"I had a spiritual awakening in my life," the participants said. "I feel that my life now has direction and purpose. I feel like I'm getting on track with where my life should have always been."

Even though I had focused on the mental and physical benefits of practicing forgiveness and had discovered that forgiveness does indeed positively impact both, the majority of the people I worked with were most thankful for the *spiritual* benefits that forgiveness gave them.

In short, what I had demonstrated in real life and supported by hard statistics was that *forgiveness has the power to bring healing to the whole person: body, mind, and spirit.*

So as you continue your journey in forgiveness, let the healing begin!

ASSIGNMENT

1. Pay attention to your body and learn to identify its weakest point. Specifically, when you experience stress, what part of your body reacts?
   a. Stomach: indigestion or irritable bowel syndrome
   b. Heart: high blood pressure or arrhythmias
   c. Headaches: tension or migraine
   d. Tiredness due to sleeplessness or chronic fatigue
   e. Other:

2. Practice forgiveness and pay close attention to any physical benefits you may notice, especially in the body part you just identified. Realize, though, that it can take up to two months for some chronic symptoms to begin to improve. Also, if you are currently experiencing physical symptoms that are causing you difficulties, review them with your physician to determine whether you have a medical condition that warrants immediate intervention.

FIVE

THE BIRTH OF A GRIEVANCE STORY

If you are distressed by anything external,
the pain is not due to the thing itself, but to your estimate of it;
and this you have the power to revoke at any moment.
—Marcus Antonius

A first-year college professor felt both elated and surprised. He had just learned that he had been assigned a class of high-achieving students, a privilege usually reserved for tenured instructors. He took to his assignment with gusto, relishing every moment with these stimulating and energetic pupils. They, in turn, responded to his enthusiasm with astonishing insights and compelling work on difficult assignments.

The professor practically lived for the hour each day he got to spend with these remarkable students. He almost dreaded the time he had to give to his other classes, with their average students, intellectual apathy, and plodding modes of thought.

At the end of the semester, the professor could hardly wait to thank the registrar for giving him such a delightful class of high achievers. So he was absolutely stunned when the registrar replied, "What are you talking about? You didn't have a class of high achievers. Those students were no different from those in any of your other classes. You must have misunderstood."

The flabbergasted young professor made a sobering discovery that day: a simple story that turned out to be untrue had the power not only to change the way he lived and thought but also to profoundly affect the students who sat in his classes.

In a similar way, the quality of your life is largely the result of the stories you believe. If your parents always told you, "You're smart! You can do anything you want to," then you probably believed that you would succeed both in school and in life. Many studies conducted over the last several years indicate that students tend to live up to the expectations others have voiced—and the process works both positively and negatively. If, for example, you were told, "You're stupid! You won't go anywhere, you moron," then you probably didn't do well in school, and you may continue to struggle in life. Why? Because you believed the story you heard over and over again and so continued to shuffle down the dreary track laid out for you by someone else.

That's why I can say that your life is profoundly influenced by the stories you believe—including the stories you tell yourself.

TALES OF HELPLESSNESS

Suppose a person offends you in some way as you're going about your daily responsibilities. What is your reaction? First, you resent the unfair treatment. You continue to think about it: *What prompted this? Why did he do that to me?* It galls you that he should be able to turn your life upside down.

Then, almost immediately, you start repeating to yourself a story that emphasizes the negative features of the event. This story—what I call a grievance story—fuels your hostility toward the person who offended you. The reason you construct your grievance story is to gain a sense of both meaning and a degree of control in life. This process, however, inevitably leads you down a self-destructive path. As you repeat and listen to this story over and over again, you convince yourself that your life is miserable and there's nothing you can do about it. You feel trapped, and every time you think of the upsetting event and the person who hurt you—every time you recall the memory—you experience the original anger all over again.

Clearly, your grievance story hurts you much more than it helps you. Therefore, if you are ever to escape the trap of victimization, you must tell yourself a different story. You must follow the advice of the ancient proverb that says, "Never repeat old grievances."

Enter forgiveness. Forgiveness allows you to reframe your story, thus changing its essence, enabling you to see events from a different perspective, and leading you to a healthier and more satisfying life.

HOW YOUR STORY TAKES SHAPE

You will learn how to reframe a grievance story later in this chapter, but for now let's consider the four stages by which every grievance story takes shape.

1. You suffer some kind of wrong.

Something happened to you that you don't like. Maybe it was an unkind comment. Perhaps it was a broken promise or an unexpected loss. Whatever it was, you think of it as unfair.

2. You attach a specific interpretation to the event.

As you feel the hurt, resentment will start to well up inside you, and you begin to blame the offender for how you feel. *This was no accident,* you think. *She did this deliberately. And she doesn't even care!* The offense becomes almost secondary to the meaning you assign to it, namely, that the person intended to hurt you.

3. You take the offense personally.

Whatever your loss, you feel it deeply. That person hurt a vital aspect of your life. Grievance stories always involve things that you consider very important; they rarely concern trivial matters.

Naturally, then, you feel the pain deeply—but you take it one step further. In fact, you begin to exaggerate the personal nature of the offense. *He targeted me,* you think. *And he knew exactly what he was doing to me and how much it would hurt.*

As you continue to ponder the hurtful incident, you increasingly emphasize its personal aspect. It wasn't merely an impersonal offense that somehow managed to injure you, an innocent bystander. No, it was a deliberate attack, a planned assault, a vindictive mugging intentionally directed at *you.*

4. You retell the story to yourself and to others.

You repeat the story, again and again, in all kinds of settings, and to all sorts of people. You also continually rehearse the story in your head. By repeatedly telling and retelling the story, you try to make some sense of the unjust event. You try to explain it, to dissect it, to lay bare the evil motivations and wicked forces behind the hurt you're suffering.

And exactly how long do you keep the story alive, repeating it to others and to yourself? Well, you keep rehearsing it either until the offender changes and makes things right or until justice is served. In other words, you keep repeating the story until the score gets evened, the books get balanced, and life becomes fair once more. Until then, the story lives on. And most people's story lives on much longer than is necessary or even helpful. Sadly, the story stays with some folks an entire lifetime.

THE PROBLEM WITH GRIEVANCE STORIES

Despite popular opinion, time does not heal all wounds. Each time you mentally rehearse your grievance story, you reopen the old wound. You remain stuck in that story, and that same old, painful script continues to guide your whole life. In fact, your story could have you suffering as long as you live.

When you refuse to forgive, you are in effect handcuffing yourself to the person who offended you, to a person you don't even like. And you know the worst thing about that? While you wait for that person to unlock the cuffs, you are holding the key in your own hands.

The truth is, only you can set yourself free, and you do that by forgiving. Forgiveness may feel like you're letting the other person off the hook, but in reality you are letting *yourself* off the hook.

Think about the "Drop the Rock" story from the beginning of the book. Unforgiveness is like carrying around a red-hot rock with the intention of throwing it at the person who caused you the hurt. But as you wait—and many folks wait for a very long time—the sizzling rock burns and scars your hand. Wouldn't it be wiser just to let the rock fall to the ground? Forgiveness is the skill of letting go. After all, as Confucius wisely observed, "To be wronged is nothing unless you continue to remember it."

Since forgiveness frees you, the forgiver, it benefits you far more than it does the person who hurt you. As long as you take the role of victim and hold on to resentment, you hold on to the person who harmed you. And is that really the person you want to live with for the rest of your life? Does that person care enough about you to act on your behalf and help free you from being trapped by your grievance story? Probably not. Forgiveness has the ability to free you from the power over your life that person has held.

NURSING A GRUDGE TAKES ENERGY

Most of us hold on to grudges because we either consciously or unconsciously believe that our grudge hurts the one who injured us or at least puts us back in control. We tend to minimize the enormous amount of energy we actually invest in holding on to our grudges. Consider what grudges actually do to us. They:

1. *Consume our lives.* We end up spending more time focusing on the grudge than we do on living productively.

2. *Deplete our energy which could be used for more important activities.* The more energy we spend holding on to a grudge, the less en-

ergy we have to spend on things that enrich our lives and bring us joy. It is not the unfair event that keeps us miserable, but our grudge. Do you really want to waste your energy, or do you want to put it to good use?

3. *Make us repeatedly feel the old pain.* Our word *resent* comes from a French term meaning "to feel again." Grudges do little to punish the offender, but they do a great job of causing us to repeatedly feel the pain the offender originally caused us. As William H. Walton rightly said, "To carry a grudge is like being stung to death by a single bee."

I have listened to many men and women tell their grievance stories with such energy, tears, and emotional fervor that I say, "Wow! We need to do something about this! That's terrible! When did it happen?"

Then they tell me, "Oh, it didn't just happen. It happened thirty years ago."

Think of it! Thirty years later they're still back where they were; they're still stuck in that same miserable place. Meanwhile, the other person has long since moved on. That's the central point to understand about a grievance story: it keeps you stuck in a dark and painful spot while the offender goes on with life. And that reality seems even more unfair than the original hurtful act.

To consider more closely your own grievance story and how it's affecting you, I recommend that you now turn to the end of this chapter and take the "Grievance Story Toxicity" self-test found there. Once you have a better handle on your own grievance story, come back here and learn how to more effectively deal with it.

THE ELEMENTS OF A GRIEVANCE STORY

Every grievance story has two significant ingredients baked right into it. Once you understand this, you can start to change both your story and your life.

1. I see my story as reality.

We see our own grievance stories as nothing less than absolutely factual reports of reality: "This is the terrible thing that happened to me. I want you to know about it so you can understand my situation and empathize with my tragic circumstances."

When we tell our stories, we believe that we're just telling the truth. We want other people to know the facts of what happened so they'll understand why we are the way we are. ("Hey, we didn't choose to be this way. Someone else pushed us into it!")

2. Someone else controls my story.

And that leads us to the second point: Who's the primary character in my grievance story? Who's the chief actor who makes this story what it is?

It's not me. It's the other person. *He's* the one exercising the most control over my life. *She's* the one who did the wrong and caused me such pain. I hold on to the belief that the people who made the mess have to fix it—and there's not a thing I can do about it until they change or apologize or do something to make my life better.

Since the main character in your grievance story is the one who hurt you, you live with that person 24/7. In fact, you find yourself stuck in that story and with that person. Your grievance story blames the offender for your own emotional needs, so you're requiring the other person to change before you can feel better.

Do you see how, in a very subtle way, your own grievance story hopelessly traps you? As long as you keep telling yourself the sad tale of how someone else messed up your life, that person remains in control and you remain stuck—and if you always tell yourself what you have always told yourself, you will always feel what you have always felt. You can't get out of it. And that, by definition, is a trap.

So can you spring yourself from this trap? Yes, you definitely can—but only when you stop dwelling on what others have done to you. They certainly are responsible for their actions, but these individuals are not responsible for how you feel about them now or what you do with your life from this point forward. No matter what has happened in the past, you are responsible for the present. In short, you need to take control of your life.

MOVE TOWARD TRUTH

So how do I free myself from the power this grievance story has over my life? The only way to get free of that trap is to change the story.

"But I can't do that!" you protest. "How can I change what happened? I won't lie about what occurred. The facts are the facts. Besides, how would manipulating and falsifying the facts about the incident change what I feel? I'll still know the truth."

Fortunately, forgiveness doesn't require you to lie to yourself in order to get unstuck from your past. Forgiveness also doesn't ask you to whitewash what happened or pretend that it doesn't really matter. In fact, forgiveness requires exactly the opposite. It doesn't ask you to forget the truth, but to remember it more fully. Forgiveness does its work best when the story you tell grows more accurate, not less. I'll lead you more fully in the revision process of your grievance story in chapter 8, but right now, keep two things in mind as you consider revising your story in the direction of truth.

1. Your grievance story is not a tale of reality.

The grievance story you tell yourself is not "the truth, the whole truth, and nothing but the truth." Far from it! It is actually riddled with distortions, biases, incomplete details, and conveniently omitted facts. Your grievance story hurts you not because it is true, but because it contains so much that is false. It traps you not because it is accurate, but because it offers a warped version of reality.

It's most likely that the incident did not happen exactly as you recall it. Your version, in fact, is not the whole story. You can't remember everything that happened to you in all its detail. You remember only those things that fit the story you have constructed. Like everyone else, you have a selective memory. Read any police report. The different versions of the same event would suggest that each witness actually saw a completely different crime. The stories can be that different.

To better understand this, picture your memory being like an iceberg. The present is the ice that shows above the surface, and stored memories comprise the huge, icy mass just under the surface. You see what lies above water, but your brain processes what you see in a relationship to everything below the surface. Consequently, you relate to people in the present through the eyes of your past experiences.

After all—and you may not know this—your mind stores memories by categories around clusters of either feelings or similar experiences from your past. You use past events to interpret current circumstances. This process can be helpful when it allows you to integrate new experiences with past ones. In that case, learning is cumulative: each new experience builds upon previous experiences. Using the past to interpret the present becomes a problem, however, when you see each new experience *only* as a repetition of some past experience. In this case, you merely reinforce old experiences and give yourself little opportunity for new learning. When some new offense occurs, you don't see it as new and unique. Rather, you think of it merely as the same awful thing that happened to you last month, last year, last decade. And you feel the same way now as you did back then.

And feelings from the past can be as potent as anything in the present. Actors draw upon this principle to bring authenticity to a character. They tap into their own experiences that resonate with those of the character they are playing, and then they reexperience those past feelings in the present. A grievance story institutionalizes this process and causes you to live in the past. Your story makes sure that you feel those old emotions, with the same intensity you did originally, whenever something remotely similar happens in the present.

The very nature of memory—the fact that memories are incomplete and perhaps even inaccurate—provides yet another opportunity for distortions in your grievance story and your view of others. (For example, not every man is like that no-good husband who left you in such a terrible predicament. I hope I'm not sounding too defensive, but some men really do care.) Furthermore, our emotional reactions to an event can be stronger than the event merited. After all, we feel negative emotions four to ten times more strongly than we feel positive ones, and that means we tend to magnify the negative aspects of what happened to us and discount the good things. We simply select the information that reinforces our beliefs while ignoring other evidence. We, in effect, choose our memories.

We human beings also struggle with what has been called "the magnitude gap." That phrase refers to the difference in perspective various individuals have of the same event. Victims exaggerate the severity of the event, downplay their own responsibility, and see the offense as damaging their future. The offenders, however, minimize the same event, increase the other's responsibility, and see the offense as primarily over and in the past. So your story of the same event will be much different from the one the offender tells.

Most victims also believe that they are owed more than the offender is willing to pay. When you've been hurt, you focus on everything negative about the incident. So you believe that something greater, something big, has to be done to even the score. You will believe that those who have hurt you owe you more than they believe they owe you, so the debt can never be paid in full.

All of these factors work together in a grievance story to distort what actually happened, to make the negative appear much larger than it might have been originally. A grievance story takes a negative event and distorts it into something far worse than the reality that sparked the account.

When I teach forgiveness seminars, I often illustrate this point by describing a minor car accident in which one vehicle bumps the fender of the car in front of it. At that point I stop the story and ask for two volunteers to come forward and role-play what happens next. One participant plays the driver who was hit, and the other plays the driver who did the hitting.

Invariably the guy in front says, "The dummy behind me wasn't watching where he was going and slammed into the back of me." To that, the guy in back responds, "I was driving behind this person who didn't know where he was going. Suddenly he slammed on his brakes for no good reason. Still, I barely touched him."

Depending on your viewpoint—whether you're the offender or the offended—you have a biased way of interpreting what happened. A grievance story picks out the details that reinforce the theme of your grievance story, which is "I'm innocent and a fine person, but you are a terrible person who did a terrible thing."

Here's the bottom line: your grievance story—more than the person who hurt you—is the enemy responsible for defeating you. And your story defeats you by constantly feeding you a collection of distortions that it passes off as the truth.

2. Your grievance story supports evil motives that you cannot verify.

When someone hurts you, where does your mind first go? If you're typical, you immediately ask, *Why did that person do that to me?* You look for motive, and if you judge the other person's motives as evil—which you usually do—then you magnify the negative impact of the hurtful behavior.

But how accurate do such judgments about motives tend to be? Not very. After all, you can observe an act, but you can never know for sure the real motive behind it. At best, you can only make a guess as to why people do what they do. This is why we are warned, "Do not judge, or you too will be judged." Besides, you can hardly identify your own motives, so how can you pretend to get in someone else's head and determine his or her motives?

The sad truth is that we all suffer from a basic human tendency toward self-serving biases. We tend to attribute our own negative behavior to *external* causes (if you're old enough, perhaps you can still hear the late comedian Flip Wilson insisting in his shrill Geraldine voice, "The devil made me do it!") while attributing the negative behavior of others to exclusively *internal* causes ("That person just likes to hurt people"). When you attribute evil motives to other people, your anger inevitably gains the upper hand.

So if you really do want to change the story that's been hurting you, you must stop attributing exclusively evil motives to the offender. You can't know what motivated the person who hurt you, and you will find it much easier to forgive once you stop assuming your own omniscience. You *don't* know what prompted the hurtful act, so stop pretending that you do.

Now do you see why your grievance story doesn't tell the whole truth? It actually offers a very distorted point of view—and it's that very often unintended distortion that causes you so much pain. So how do you change your grievance story to better reflect reality?

CHANGE YOUR PERSPECTIVE

It would be nice if you could simply erase your story and be rid of it. Unfortunately, deep hurts do not disappear that easily. Forgetting the unpleasant event is not even an option, for it just can't be done. As psychiatrist Thomas Szasz put it, "The stupid neither forgive nor forget; the naive forgive and forget; the wise forgive but do not forget." The goal of forgiveness is to remember in a different way.

Forgiveness challenges you to change the way you think and to minimize the distortions that warp your view of reality. In short, what you have been telling yourself is not only inaccurate, but it is causing you to act and think in ways that sabotage your own growth and well-being. In order for forgiveness to be most effective, it must revise and correct the inaccurate story you have been telling yourself.

Truth and reality are the only effective cures for healing the distortions of a grievance story, distortions that you originally developed to explain your hurt and anger. Then forgiveness helps you accept that truth and reality. The following two interventions provide a good starting place for this life-changing process.

1. Evaluate the incident more carefully.

Forgiveness challenges you to consider how important this one event really is in the big picture of all that's going on in your life and in the world. In most grievance stories, the hurtful incident overshadows every other life experience. But would a neutral party assign it that much importance? Probably not.

This is not to say that a single event cannot feel overwhelming and have a dramatic impact on your life; a single event certainly can. But even incidents with enormously far-reaching consequences will impact people differently. The tragic events of 9-11, for instance, did not affect everyone the same way. The terrorist attacks on the Twin Towers in New York and the Pentagon in Washington killed thousands and left a nation in mourning. Yet not everyone who lost a loved one that day responded in the same manner. Some grieved, picked up the pieces of their life, and courageously moved on. Others have held on to their bitterness and rage and not moved an inch since that terrible day. People in both categories had to deal with the same reality of their loss, but they did so in very different ways.

So evaluate the incident that's at the core of your grievance story. Ask yourself, "Is my lot in life really determined by another person's hurtful actions, or do I have a say about how my life will be affected—both now and in the future?" Forgiveness places control of your life back into your hands, reminding you to take action that is for your good. Remember, forgiving is for your benefit.

2. Act—don't react.

Learn to be an actor, not a reactor. Actors can enjoy life because they make it what they want it to be, but reactors must take life as it comes to them.

When we react to other people, we join their dance—and why dance with a person you don't like? Forgiveness allows you to stand on the side and watch them dance. You don't have to dance with them if you don't want to. You can dance the dance you enjoy with whomever you enjoy.

Forgiveness fosters a willingness to recognize that the insensitive or negative behavior of others is an expression of something missing or inadequate in their life. In fact, forgiveness has more to do with recognizing the other person's needs and shortcomings than your own personal injuries. Maybe the one who hurt you fears rejection, failure, or not being in control. These fears then get displayed in negative, controlling, or irresponsible behavior. The bottom line: the other person's inappropriate behavior is a survival mechanism that kicks in when that person's needs are not met. In short, since their behavior is their issue, you should not allow it to become your consequence.

These interventions—evaluating the incident more carefully and acting rather than reacting—will help you focus on the real issue: who's responsible for your life? Is it the person who hurt you, or is it you? Your answer to this question will determine if you are free to live your life or if you are trapped in the web another has laid for you.

SET YOURSELF FREE

Forgiveness is the way to take back control of your life. Once you adopt a forgiving perspective, your grievance story will begin to lose its power to hurt you, and you will gladly welcome the new way of life that follows. You will live a happier and healthier life once you accept these potent truths:

- Holding on to your anger hurts only you.

- When you forgive, you set a prisoner free—and that prisoner is you.

- When you change for the better, people around you can more easily change for the better.

Why allow the past—or, more accurately, your distorted memory of the past—to continue to both damage your present and derail your future? You deserve better. So why not let go of what hurts and reach for what helps? Why not, in other words, *choose forgiveness*?

ASSIGNMENT

Picture someone you're angry with but are willing to forgive. Clearly call to mind both the person and the hurtful situation. Then take a few deep breaths and answer the following questions about this person and the hurtful incident.

1. Try retelling the grievance story by placing yourself in charge of your life. What can you do differently to reduce that person's power over you? If that course of action seems reasonable, try it.

2. In what ways is this incident keeping you from living a rewarding and enjoyable life? What do you need to do differently so that you will be free of the past and start investing in your future?

3. How long ago did this event happen? If it's been more than a year, you might consider getting some extra help from someone you trust so that you can process your emotions and thoughts in order to successfully move on with your life.

GRIEVANCE STORY TOXICITY

Think of an injustice done to you, the most troublesome or painful incident you can recall. This is your grievance story. Perhaps you have already resolved it. If so, think about how you felt at the time of the incident. If your story has not been resolved, then answer the questions based on how you feel today. Your answers to these questions should give you a clear picture of how your grievance story is affecting you.

To get the best results from this test, don't answer according to what you think you *should* believe or feel. Instead, respond based on what is actually true for you. The more honest you are with yourself, the more meaningful the results of this test will be.

Answer the following questions by placing a checkmark in the appropriate column:

                                          A   B   C

1. How long ago did the events of my
   grievance story occur?   ___ ___ ___
   a. Within the last year
   b. Within the last one to five years
   c. More than five years ago

2. How frequently do I think of this story? ___ ___ ___
   a. Monthly to yearly
   b. Weekly to monthly
   c. Daily to weekly

3. Whom do I blame for what happened? ___ ___ ___
   a. I don't need to blame.
   b. I blame the other person.
   c. I blame myself.

4. Why do I think the other person did this to me?___ ___ ___
   a. That person had limited skills and abilities.
   b. That person is bad—and mean to everyone.
   c. That person was out to get me personally.

5. I retell the story in my mind with the goal of: ___ ___ ___
   a. Learning from it in order to grow.
   b. Getting the other person to change and recognize his or
      her fault.
   c. To punish the other person for what he or she did.

6. What feeling do I have as I tell my story?   — — —
   a. Determination
   b. Anger
   c. Helplessness

7. Each time I retell my story, I: — — —
   a. Learn from it.
   b. Further develop my plan for vengeance.
   c. Become more overwhelmed.

8. The person with the most power in my
   story is: — — —
   a. Me
   b. Someone else
   c. The one who offended me

9. To improve my current circumstances: — — —
   a. I need to take action to achieve my
      goals.
   b. Justice needs to be served against the
      one who offended me.
   c. The offender needs to apologize and
      change.

10. Have I contemplated forgiveness before?   — — —
    a. I forgave this person, and the situation
       no longer bothers me.
    b. I tried to forgive but was unable to.
    c. I immediately dismissed the thought
       because the person who hurt me did
       not deserve forgiveness.

SCORING

Checkmarks in the A column are worth 0 points.
Each checkmark in the B column is worth 1 point.
Each checkmark in the C column is worth 2 points.

Add your total points for all ten questions and then look at the scoring guide below to determine the toxicity of your grievance story.

If your score was between:

- 0–5—You appear to be processing your grievance in a healthy way that allows you to learn from the past and go on with your life.

- 6–10—You have some difficulty working through past offenses, and you may be giving the offender(s) too much power and control in your life.

- 11–20—You are likely overwhelmed by what has happened to you. You should consider seeking assistance from a friend or professional who can help you get free of the trap of victimization.

SIX

FORGIVENESS IS A CHOICE

The only freedom that cannot be taken away is the freedom of choice.
—Victor Frankl

As a young man in his thirties, Simon Wiesenthal found himself a prisoner in a Nazi concentration camp. The extraordinarily harsh conditions of the camp made him envy the dead Germans whose graves he saw decorated with sunflowers.

One day a dying Nazi soldier asked for a Jew—any Jew—to be summoned to his bedside. Soldiers yanked Wiesenthal from his work detail and took him to the mortally wounded man, who regretfully confessed his awful crimes, including the murder of a young child along with the child's entire family. Then the soldier asked a shocking question: would Wiesenthal forgive him for what he did?

Whether out of surprise, revulsion, fear, bitterness, or something else entirely, Wiesenthal remained silent. Not long afterward, the conscience-stricken German soldier died without receiving the forgiveness he had so urgently sought.

Years after his liberation from that death camp, Wiesenthal continued to wonder whether he had done the right thing. Should he have forgiven the murderous soldier? The question becomes a great deal thornier when you realize that the Nazis had murdered eighty-nine members of Wiesenthal's family, including his wife's relatives.

Eventually Wiesenthal wrote *The Sunflower: On the Possibilities and Limits of Forgiveness*. After telling his own horrific story, he wrote, "You, who have just read this sad and tragic episode in my life, can YOU mentally change places with me and ask yourself the crucial question: 'What would I have done?'"

Would *you* have made the same choice that Simon Wiesenthal did? The book's publishers put that question to fifty-three prominent individuals—theologians, jurists, psychiatrists, Holocaust survivors, escapees of genocides in Bosnia, Cambodia, and elsewhere, and personalities such as the Dalai Lama, former Nazi Albert Speer, Rabbi Harold Kushner, and talk-show personality Dennis Prager. All of them weighed in on what they saw as the proper response. Some say yes to forgiveness, while others say no.

It all boils down to a choice, doesn't it? To forgive or not to forgive—that really is the question.

THE POWER TO CHOOSE

Respect for human dignity requires that we see each individual as endowed with the ability to make choices. Throughout history, great leaders, celebrated thinkers, and everyday folks have all acknowledged the crucial role of personal choice.

- "It's choice—not chance—that determines your destiny," declared Jean Nidetch.

- "Nothing is more difficult, and therefore more precious, than to be able to decide," stated Napoleon Bonaparte.

- "One ship sails East,
  And another West,
  By the self-same winds that blow,
  'Tis the set of the sails
  And not the gales,
  That tells the way we go."— Ella Wheeler Wilcox

- "What we call the secret of happiness is no more a secret than our willingness to choose life," said Leo Buscaglia.

The freedom to choose—the power of choice—confronts you every time you are wronged. Will you choose blame? Or will you choose forgiveness? Will you hand over the reins of your life to someone you don't even like, or will you decide to direct the path of your own future?

What will you choose?

Before you can begin to enjoy any of the profound benefits of forgiveness, you must choose to forgive. This decision, however halfhearted it may initially be, is key to taking your first step toward freedom. And you do have the power to choose to forgive the one who hurt you.

STIMULUS—PAUSE—RESPONSE

"But," some may wonder, "do we really have the ability to choose how we react to unpleasant circumstances? Doesn't Psychology 101 teach us that basic human behaviors are largely determined by a variety of stimuli that trigger our responses?"

Yes, that's exactly what some psychologists teach. We can illustrate the basic process like this:

STIMULUS → RESPONSE

This process suggests that your responses are mostly determined by the circumstances that impact your life. We come to believe that our circumstances are the result of someone else's actions. In essence: you act and I react. This reaction forms your grievance story which states: "My crummy circumstances are the result of what someone else has done to me." In other words, "My life is your fault."

I would like to take the opposite position and suggest that, for humans, a brief pause occurs between stimulus and response. During this brief pause we can either react to the stimulus, or we can reflect on our available choices and determine how we will respond. In our current discussion, for instance, you can choose forgiveness or revenge. The choice is yours.

I believe this moment of reflection is what makes us truly human and is the point where we come into closest contact with our soul or spiritual nature. As we reflect, we draw upon our values, morals, and core beliefs about what is right and true. The choices we make during this reflective moment define our character and help shape who we truly are. The choices we make today determine who we will become tomorrow.

Therefore, a more accurate portrayal of how a thoughtful individual can make choices would look like this:

STIMULUS → REFLECTION → RESPONSE

Clearly, you do not have to react in an automatic, predetermined way when something happens to you that you don't like. Even if you begin to react in an unhealthy way, you can choose to stop that reaction and instead focus on options that will benefit you rather than harm you. It's all about the choices you make.

And your choices are shaped not so much by the event itself, but by your interpretation of that event. And, as we have seen, your recollection and your interpretation of certain facts shape and form your story. Therefore, by changing your interpretation of the event, you create a wider range of responses from which to select.

THE ELEMENTS OF CHOICE

Choice is a complex matter. In fact, the choices we make usually depend on some combination of the following factors.

1. *Intentionality about a desired result*

Normally we don't make choices arbitrarily. We select one course of action over another because we believe that choice will benefit us more than the other available options will. By making that particular choice, we intend to move ourselves toward something we prefer or value. And I maintain that the choice to forgive moves us closer to health and satisfaction than the choice not to forgive.

2. Belief that the goal is attainable

No sane person hops on a bicycle believing that he or she can pedal to Jupiter. Likewise, we choose courses of action that we believe really have a chance—however slim—of accomplishing what will bring us some measure of satisfaction. And I maintain that the option to forgive really is possible, even in the most difficult of circumstances.

3. Actions that make your intentions reality

Choices are more than mere wishes. After all, a wish is a desire for beneficial results without any effort to obtain those results. I might wish I could play jazz on my saxophone, but if I don't choose to practice daily and learn the required skills, my wish remains nothing more than a pipe dream. A choice, however, implies the determination to act. And I maintain that choosing to forgive means taking specific, concrete actions that give your forgiveness "legs" (a topic we'll discuss in detail in coming chapters).

4. The desire to minimize internal conflict with core values and competing desires

We generally make choices that are consistent with our most deeply held beliefs and strongest values. We tend to hesitate in our decision making when we feel caught in a cross fire between competing values and desires. When few or none of these internal battles take place, it is simply easier to make a decision. So if we know in advance that forgiveness is a healthier choice than vengeance, there will be less uncertainty about which path to take when we're confronted with an undesirable situation.

5. Consideration of the impact your current actions will have on your future goals

Few of us would choose to make our futures dark or tough or painful. So we need to consider whether a choice we make today is likely to benefit us in the long run or whether that choice will doom our tomorrows. We all want to create the brightest future possible for ourselves, so we generally choose whatever option seems most likely to get us there. And I maintain that forgiveness grants you, by far, the best chance of reaching your most cherished goals.

In short, you decide your destiny by the daily choices you make. As I've said, your choices—and that includes the choice to forgive —make you the person you are.

WHICH ROAD LOOKS BETTER?

So when something undesirable happens to you because of another person's actions, you must decide between forgiveness and unforgiveness. To refuse to forgive is a choice just as clearly as your choice to forgive is. Which is the better choice for you?

Whenever you come face-to-face with an upsetting experience, I suggest that you ask yourself these three critical questions:

1. Is the hurtful experience worth sacrificing my peace of mind?

2. How much space in my mind am I willing to set aside for this person I don't even like?

3. Am I sufficiently focused on my life goals so as not to allow this event to distract me from what is truly important to me?

If you are spending more time plotting how to get even rather than how to let go and move on, then you are not choosing to forgive. If you are spending more time examining the hurt rather than healing it, then you are not choosing to forgive. If you are spending more time trying to change the past rather than improve your future, then you are not choosing to forgive.

Even when you decide that forgiveness really is the best option for you, other choices follow. One of the more critical decisions you will need to make is whether *now* is the right time for forgiveness.

FORGIVE WHEN YOU'RE READY

There is no fixed timetable for when you must forgive a wrong done to you. No one can tell you when to forgive. You alone make the decision to forgive; you alone will know when you are ready. And you may not be ready to forgive. That's OK, but don't shut forgiveness off as a future option.

Even when you do choose to forgive, you can stop the process any time should the pain become too intense. Then later, when you feel more ready, you can choose to start the process of forgiveness again.

Remember, forgiveness is a choice; it's your choice. Forgiveness does not happen automatically or when someone else thinks or even insists it should. Forgiveness cannot be forced; no one can compel you to forgive, nor should you allow anyone to make you feel guilty for not forgiving. You can forgive only if you want to, and you will want to only when you recognize that the price you are paying by *not* forgiving is greater than what you would lose by forgiving.

Again, the right time to forgive is when you're ready, not a moment before. After all, you *cannot* forgive unless you choose to, and that decision should only happen when you are ready.

KEEP YOUR OPTIONS OPEN

As with any choice, you must weigh your options and select the one that gives you the best chance to get you where you most want to be. And I personally believe that when someone hurts you, forgiveness is always a better choice than not forgiving, for the potential benefits of forgiveness far outweigh the steep price you pay by refusing to forgive.

The most important point here is to place forgiveness on your list of options. If you don't even recognize forgiveness as an option, you will never choose to forgive. I know of many people who refuse to even consider forgiveness a viable option. Don't make that mistake! Forgiveness is *always* an option.

In the end, you'll make good choices and bad choices throughout your life; everyone does. But when you make a bad choice, you can always go back and review it. You can think about how you made that decision and how it is affecting you. By doing so, you can learn and grow and then make healthier choices in the future. Also keep in mind that even a bad choice can usually be compensated for with a good choice.

Again, unless you keep forgiveness on your radar screen, a choice to be made when you are ready, you will never choose to forgive. And, as we've seen, that choice can have serious consequences.

I know it's not always easy to do, but choosing forgiveness is almost certainly the best option for getting you where you want to be in life. If you want to live with freedom and joy, at some point you must choose to forgive.

Choose a Better Way

You have seen how the old strategies of planning your revenge and retelling your grievance story simply don't work. You realize there has to be a better way, a way that will move you away from powerlessness and pain.

Forgiveness is that better way.

Of course you'll often have to choose to forgive even when you don't feel like forgiving—but never give up your ability to choose! If you relinquish that option, you become a victim, and we've seen that victims have no choices. They simply end up allowing others to determine their circumstances. Victims blame the people around them for who they have become—and as these victims complain about their miserable life, they fail to recognize that they do in fact have the ability to choose a different life for themselves. So a victim remains stuck in the past. In sharp contrast, a victor learns from the past and then moves toward a desired future.

You may not have always had the ability or been in circumstances that allowed you to make good choices. As a child, for instance, you were tied to your parents and did not always have the opportunity to make healthy choices. For example, if your parents hit and even beat you whenever they had too much to drink, you may have had to live more in fear than in hope. In that case you made choices out of fear, choices that helped you avoid hurt rather than pursue happiness. As an adult, however, you can choose to remain bound by those who hurt you—your parents, spouse, boss, or some other authority figure—or you can forgive them and thereby free yourself from their domination.

Forgiveness frees you to make the ultimate choice in life: will you choose to be a victim or a victor?

CHOOSE LIFE!

You can choose to forgive—the path of life—or you can choose not to forgive—the path of death. But a lot of people I meet never frame the situation in those terms. They don't choose *not* to forgive; they simply don't forgive.

"I guess I'm a little like that," you comment. "I never made a conscious choice not to forgive. I just have never forgiven the person who hurt me so deeply."

Please understand that by not specifically choosing to forgive, you are choosing not to forgive. The alternative, however, is always there: you could choose to forgive. In fact, you could make that choice today or tomorrow, for the window of opportunity to forgive never closes. So I challenge you today to carefully consider the option of forgiveness.

To forgive or not to forgive; that is the question.

What choice will you make?

ASSIGNMENT

1. When you're confronted with an undesirable situation, is for-giveness an option you regularly consider? Why or why not?

2. Before reacting to another person's hurtful actions or words, take some time to list all the possible responses you can think of. Then, beside each possibility, note the consequences of each option if you were to select that one. This exercise will strengthen your ability to make the best choice.

3. Think about someone you have not forgiven. Was that a con-scious choice or a natural response to being hurt? What can you do to make that choice more conscious?

4. Can you forgive that person at this time? Do you want to for-give that person? Is forgiving that person, or *not* forgiving that person, the better choice for you? Consider the consequences of both choices. What effect would the choice to forgive or *not* to forgive have on you?

SEVEN

IT'S NOT EASY
TO FORGIVE

The greatest discovery of my generation
is that a human being can alter his life by altering his attitude.
—William James

Ifondly remember Kermit the Frog singing from his heart "It's Not Easy Bein' Green." His musical lament came to mind as I was thinking about how difficult forgiveness can be. To almost quote Kermit, it's not easy to forgive. And this sentiment gets expressed in so many different ways:

"I try to forgive, but I just can't."

"I know I should forgive, but I just don't feel like it."

"I don't get why he did that to me. I would never do anything like that to him!"

These are some of the reasons people find it difficult to forgive, but the greatest barrier to forgiveness is our inability to understand why someone would intentionally hurt us. Even when we choose to forgive, this lack of understanding may cause us to struggle with actually forgiving the offender. We want to forgive; we know we should forgive; we decide to forgive . . . but we hesitate when our wounded feelings get in the way.

What can we do about feelings that run counter to our desire to forgive? In other words, is there any way to deal with these feelings so that it's easier to forgive? Thankfully, the answer is yes. Two key characteristics make forgiveness more likely to occur, and they are *humility* and *empathy*.

CHARACTERISTIC ONE: HUMILITY

The English word *humility* comes from the Latin *humilitas*, which in turn is derived from humus, referring to dirt or soil. Dirt can be seen either as the lowest thing on earth or as that from which all life springs. As I see it, forgiveness—like good soil—is also a source of life. And, interestingly, the most forgiving people I know are also the most humble.

But what exactly is humility?

A PROPER VIEW OF SELF

Standing in the way of humility is our need to be important. Within every single one of us is an inner longing for personal significance. Everyone you'll ever meet (and that includes you) aspires to be somebody; no one wants to be a nobody. But must we always talk about our successes in order to be recognized as important? Or, conversely, do we have to hide our failures for fear that they will diminish our significance as a person? For the humble person, the answer to both questions is a resounding no.

In fact, humility is the ability to balance one's successes and accomplishments with one's failures and shortcomings. Contrary to what many think, being humble doesn't mean being a nobody; it just means you don't try to be more of a somebody than you ought to be.

To be humble doesn't mean degrading yourself or considering yourself less than everyone else. Instead, being humble means having an accurate picture of who you really are—warts, dimples, and every trait in between. To be humble is not to have a low opinion of yourself, but to see yourself as no better or worse than the other person. The terms *unpretentious* and *modest* more accurately describe a humble person than such terms as *self-effacing* or *self-deprecating*.

Humility not only allows you to see others as equal to yourself, but it also requires you to see yourself as equal to others. This awareness actually paves the way for forgiveness to take place, for the one who wronged you is no longer so very different from you. Instead, that person becomes more like you. After all, humble people recognize that, under the right set of circumstances, they are quite capable of causing another person the kind of terrible hurt they themselves have experienced.

The truly humble also feel secure in their personal identity. They don't depend on the opinions of others to give them significance. They know that identity is not what others give them but what they give themselves, so they feel free to explore and grow in ways they desire. Ralph Waldo Emerson put it this way: "To be yourself in a world that is constantly trying to make you something else is the greatest accomplishment."

Confidence is not synonymous with beating down the other guy, but with knowing who you are and becoming what you believe you are meant to be.

STRONG, NOT WEAK

Contrary to popular opinion, humility is a sign of strength, not weakness. We are reminded of this truth every time we observe insecure people who need to constantly talk about how great they are. They are not displaying their strength but their inner weakness; for eventually that false front becomes evident. When people try to be more than they are, they display their weakness. They may appear strong, but they are actually weak. In contrast, the strength of humble people becomes apparent in their inner confidence and genuine strength of character. When they are no more or no less than who they are, they show their strength. They do not need to constantly prove themselves. Their actions speak louder than their words.

Because of their inner strength, humble people can be vulnerable and open with others. After all, they have nothing to hide. And because they are comfortable with who they are, they have no interest in taking advantage of others in order to improve their own situation. They don't need to make me appear weak so they can look strong. They already are strong and secure in their own identity. That's one reason why they can be with me in my pain and suffering: they have no need to deny their own struggles. They have been there and survived, a fact that can be very encouraging to me when I'm struggling.

Yes, I like humble people. They feel safe to be around, I feel better about myself when I hang around them, and I have less of a need to compete because they give me so much support. In fact, the more I'm around humble people, the more I want to become like them.

WE ALL MAKE MISTAKES

We all make mistakes, and humility reminds us to never demand perfection from those around us because they are no more perfect than you or I. "Be not angry that you cannot make others as you wish them to be," said Thomas à Kempis, "since you cannot make yourself as you wish to be."

To one degree or another, every human being acts in his or her own best interest. And what one person does in his own best interest may not be in the best interest of another. So, sooner or later, someone will suffer a hurtful offense. Why are we surprised when it happens?

Humility is the ability to face your own fallible humanness *and* appreciate the humanness of others. Humble people can see their own shortcomings, so they tend to be less demanding of other people. Also, since they know their own true potential, they more readily see the potential of others. Humble people don't get hung up on past failures, but rather have an eye toward what can be. They see possibilities where others see only failures.

Furthermore, humble individuals recognize the absurdity of saying that someone is unworthy or undeserving of forgiveness or that the mistake should never have been made in the first place. After all, who *is* worthy or deserving of forgiveness? Those who never make mistakes? If so, that pretty much excludes all of us, doesn't it?

Now think about this: How could anyone consistently say, "I've made mistakes. I'm not perfect. And I'm thankful that someone has forgiven me" yet be unwilling to extend the same courtesy to others?

So, go ahead. Admit that you have made mistakes and acknowledge that others have forgiven you. Since you have benefited from their forgiveness, shouldn't you be willing to forgive the people who hurt you? It's very freeing to accept the fact that you're not perfect, to openly confess that you make mistakes, and then to be thankful that someone was gracious enough to forgive you.

The fact is, it's much easier to forgive when you know you've been forgiven. So sometimes, as a counselor, I offer my clients forgiveness before I ask them to forgive someone else. I listen to the story and note all its pain. In any grievance story, you detect not only anger over what someone else did, but also self-blame. Listen carefully and you'll hear something like this: "I got myself into this. I didn't ask for what happened, but I made some stupid choices, and this is where I ended up. I blame myself just as much as I blame the other guy. I should have known better."

When I hear people blaming themselves for the bad choices they have made, I offer forgiveness. It is not that they need my forgiveness, but I want to model for them what they need to do for themselves. Such individuals must forgive themselves before they will ever be able to forgive anyone else. In a very real sense, humility can only take root when you have first experienced forgiveness. And who doesn't need a little forgiving now and then?

WHAT'S MY ROLE IN THIS MESS?

Humility not only allows you to accept the idea that no one (including you) is perfect, but it also allows you to take responsibility for whatever part you may have played in the painful incident. It enables you to ask, "What's my role in this mess?" and then answer your own question boldly and honestly.

As we've seen, very few offenses are 100 percent the fault of one party and zero percent the responsibility of the other. Humility enables you to see what you may have done to contribute to the hurtful incident. Of course, as in a case of spousal abuse, violence against a minor, or gross parental misconduct, this issue is not always relevant. But, in most cases, considering your responsibility in the situation can provide further perspective and even some learning about yourself.

When you look carefully at the incident through the rearview mirror, you may see things that you hadn't noticed before. Humility gives you the ability to discard a warped version of "what really happened" and instead embrace a more accurate picture of the role you played.

Holding tenaciously to the belief that you are perfect in every way will not help you achieve humility. Even when you aren't sure what you may have done to contribute to the unwanted and painful event, recognizing that your actions—intended or unintended—may have impacted the other person is a sign of humility.

HUMILITY ISN'T STUPIDITY

Now, humility doesn't mean you roll over and play dead. It doesn't mean you admit you were wrong even if you don't believe you were. Humility doesn't close its eyes to the ugly mess and pretend it's not there. It simply paves the way for you to genuinely forgive the one who hurt you.

Of course you don't have to stay in hurtful relationships. Humility is not stupidity! Genuine humility will never force you to return to an abusive relationship where you'll be bludgeoned yet again. You may be very humble and forgiving, yet choose to keep some distance between you and the one who keeps hurting you. Humility not only allows you to do this; it actually encourages that wise course of action. Humble people don't deny reality. They look reality squarely in the face and deal with it.

HUMILITY SMOOTHES THE WAY

Clearly, humility smoothes the way for forgiveness to take place. Having an accurate perspective on yourself and your own humanness makes it easier for you to forgive those who have hurt you. Humility enables you to:

- Acknowledge your own wrongdoings

- Accept your limitations

- Take responsibility for your mistakes

- Apologize for the wrongs you committed

- Graciously receive correction and feedback

- Learn from your failures

- More accurately view your own actions

- Think and say good things about others

- Rejoice over other people's success

- Count your blessings in all circumstances, good and bad

- Treat all people with respect, regardless of their past actions

Humility helps you to see that most people generally do the best they can. And you help others (as well as yourself) through the ups and downs of life by appreciating their best efforts.

Humble individuals make the effort to listen to and accept others —and the more accepting they are, the more they find themselves held in high regard. Put simply, humility is leaving space in your life for others rather than filling your life exclusively with your own concerns.

To summarize, humble people forgive because they are keenly aware of their own need for forgiveness. They view themselves as no higher or lower than others. They accept that mistakes happen, that they are just as likely to make mistakes as the next person, and that everyone's mistakes require correction and forgiveness. Humble people view disappointments as a part of life. But they learn from life's lessons and move on. That's why it's easier for them to make forgiveness a regular part of their lives.

CHARACTERISTIC TWO: EMPATHY

The word *empathy* means "to feel into," as opposed to *sympathy*, which means "to feel with." Empathy is the ability to comprehend someone else's situation without actually experiencing it.

We "feel into" their experience by asking ourselves the question "How would I feel if I were in that person's situation?" Or, better yet, we ask ourselves, "What in my experience is similar to that experience, and what did I feel when I was going through it?" While the experiences of two individuals are never exactly the same, the accompanying feelings can be quite similar. But be careful here. You should never say, "I know exactly how you feel." You can never know exactly what another person is feeling. Again, empathy is feeling "into" another person's experience rather than taking on his or her feeling.

THE CONNECTION BETWEEN EVENT AND FEELING

So why exactly does empathy give you a greater understanding of the person who hurt you? Because similar events tend to cause similar feelings. The following list shows the cause-and-effect relationship between some particular event and the corresponding feelings.

- Loss makes me sad.

- Betrayal makes me angry.

- Difficult situations make me indecisive.

- Uncertainty makes me anxious.

The exact nature and specific details of the events will vary from person to person, but the resulting feelings will be very similar. That's why you don't have to have exactly the same experience as another person in order to relate to him or her. You only need to know the general *type* of event and how it might resonate with one of your own experiences.

For example, loss can involve a relationship, an object, a job, or a dream. Clearly, some losses are greater than others. Even when the event is similar, such as the death of a pet, the emotional impact can be felt in different ways and to varying degrees. But we are more alike than we are different, so in general the resulting feeling from any loss will be similar for all of us.

Empathy enables you to step away from your own interests and compassionately see the struggles and hurts others are experiencing. You temporarily detach from your own concerns and take the perspective of the other in order to gain a greater understanding of what that person is going through.

BUT FOR THE GRACE OF GOD . . .

Native Americans offer this instruction about empathy: "Before you criticize anyone, walk a mile in his moccasins." The purpose of empathy is to understand what it would be like to experience what another person is going through.

As we've seen, when someone hurts you, you tend to see that person as fundamentally different from yourself. You tend to demonize those who have done you harm by attributing to them evil intents and negative characteristics. Empathy, however, enables you to see your offenders more like you than different from you. You can now place yourself in their circumstances and understand something of the forces at play that could have contributed to their actions. You do this not to excuse their offenses, but to stop seeing them as totally evil. You then move from "He's a total jerk" to "He was inconsiderate in this instance."

Empathy enables you to see the individual less and less as evil and in need of punishment and more and more as limited and in need of healing and growth. This perspective reduces the distance between you and your offenders. If you see nothing of yourself in the other person, you will have a harder time empathizing and, eventually, forgiving. This concept of identifying with another person's situation is captured in the statement "There but for the grace of God go I."

Remember, we human beings are more like one another than we are different. So you undoubtedly have many things in common with the people who have hurt you along the way even if you would never have acted the way they did. Gaining some understanding of why people do what they do—that's empathy—makes it easier for you to forgive them.

THREE STEPS TO DEVELOPING EMPATHY

So what can you do to increase your ability to empathize with people who hurt you? There are three primary steps to developing empathy. They are:

1. Acknowledge that you are more similar to the offender than you are different.

2. Admit your own imperfections and tendencies to hurt other people.

3. Remind yourself that everyone can grow and change.

You won't be far off if you think of empathy as seeing others the way you wish to be seen. After all, when you mess up, don't you hope that someone will empathize and take into account your difficult circumstances?

Someday you might find yourself as the offender who needs to say, "What I did was wrong, but I'm not a mean or nasty person.

I'm just weak in that area. I have some bad habits. I found myself doing something that doesn't at all represent who I am. I'm so glad that someone could see that, forgive me, and love me anyway!"

Two Words of Caution

I want to offer two words of caution here. First of all, understanding is not the same as condoning the hurtful act or granting the offender permission to do it again. It's not the same as agreeing with the person's action.

Understanding through empathy does not make a wrong action right—in fact, what the person did may be very wrong—but empathy does give you a different perspective on the person's limitations. And that brings me back to humility, for I realize that I have my own limitations.

Case in point: I hate to admit it, but I'm more like my parents than I care to admit. (My wife occasionally reminds me of this fact.) Even though I've tried to learn and grow through the years, I still have some troublesome tendencies due to my home environment and the culture in which I grew up. So I continue to act, unconsciously, in certain ways.

For example, I have a tendency to exaggerate, as did my father. Sometimes I combine ideas that, when taken together, may not be 100 percent factual. My wife calls that a lie; I call it making a point. And you know what? We're both right. My intent is not to tell a lie, but by the time I finish my tale, a "lie" is woven through it somewhere. I don't see it as a lie because, as a storyteller, I am clear with my listeners that I tend to embellish in order to make a point. The problem is that if people don't recognize when I am making a point by exaggerating the facts, they may believe everything I say. So when I do misinform someone, I hope that person tries to understand both my intent and my background. In other words, I want that person to empathize with me rather than judge me.

Empathy helps you realize that, even though some action may have hurt you, the people responsible may not have intended to cause you pain. They may simply have done something normal for them. Empathy enables you to see your offenders in a different light without condoning or excusing what they did. Although you don't like what they did, you can at least somewhat understand the circumstances that caused them to act in that way. Then you can be less harsh with them.

Now for my second caution about empathy: be careful of attempts at empathy when you don't quite connect with the other person's experience. Consider an incident that took place during Canada's 1992 election. In a speech on Vancouver's skid row, former prime minister Kim Campbell attempted to connect with her voters in the audience. So she told homeless residents that she, too, had known loss and disappointment, for she had once wanted to be a concert cellist. Not surprisingly, the speech bombed. Although Campbell had tried to communicate empathy, she used an analogy that her audience couldn't relate to at all.

So be very careful of missing the mark in your attempt to empathize with the plight of others. Even though your experiences may fall under the same general category (loss, betrayal, uncertainty, etc.), the difference in degree can make for an ineffective analogy that burns bridges rather than builds them.

Finally, never assume that you fully understand other people's circumstances. Always ask for clarification. After all, they know their own life better than you do. Whenever I offer an empathetic response, I do so tentatively in order to allow the other person to modify or correct my perspective. I try to avoid presuming anything about that person's situation. Remember, the goal of empathy is to connect with other people because, to some degree, you understand their situation and feelings.

Making Forgiveness Possible

Humility and empathy pave the way for forgiveness. As they work together, humility and empathy actually make forgiveness more likely to occur.

And why not? If I can see myself or my experience reflected in another individual, why wouldn't I treat that person the way I want to be treated? As I better understand the similarities between myself and the other person, forgiveness becomes more likely. And humility and empathy are what make that understanding possible.

Assignment

Think of someone you need to forgive and ask yourself the following questions:

1. How do I feel about that person?

2. In what ways would my life be better if I chose to forgive this person?

Now make the choice to forgive. To make the act of forgiving easier, practice empathy and humility by answering these questions:

1. Why might this person have acted as hurtfully as he or she did?

2. What fears might have prompted that action?

3. What might I have done if I were faced with similar circumstances?

EIGHT

FORGIVING BY REFRAMING THE PAST

There are lots of people who mistake their imagination for their memory.
—Josh Billings

Have you ever had the opportunity to return to the old haunts you knew and loved as a child? I have, and when I did, I found the experience both exciting and disappointing. On the one hand, it felt good to revisit my favorite spots where, in my memory, I once slew dragons and escaped danger by the slimmest of margins. On the other hand, the current reality of those places felt uncomfortably . . . uh . . . different from what I remembered.

In my mind's eye I recall climbing a giant's ladder into the hayloft over our garage where we used to build passageways as deep and long as any secret tunnel in the great pyramids of Egypt. My adult eyes, however, saw a space that could not have extended more than six bales deep.

How radically different is the perspective of a six-foot-three-inch adult from that of a four-foot-two-inch child! I think of what author John Updike has written: "In memory's telephoto lens, far objects are magnified."

I had a similar disconcerting experience in the basement of my childhood home. I remembered it as a large, underground cavern,

113

with untold miles of labyrinthine tunnels that spiraled out in every direction, leading to worlds unknown. And today? Today that basement is nothing more than a small, below-the-ground room with heating ducts crisscrossing the ceiling.

The places of my childhood will never again be the same for me. Today, armed with newer and more accurate information, I haven't forgotten those old memories, but they have been permanently changed.

Reality, I have found, is as you recall it. So I can appreciate the observation of English novelist P. D. James: "It was one of those perfect English autumnal days which occur more frequently in memory than in life."

One's memories of the past are key when it comes to forgiveness. After all, what you remember is what you need to forgive. The good news is that you don't have to stay mired in the ugly past you remember. You *can* change your pain-filled memories through the process of forgiveness. In this chapter I will show you how.

REFRAMING YOUR PAST

I call changing—modifying, correcting, adjusting—your memories "reframing your past." This concept is best understood when you consider how a frame changes your perspective on a picture. A small frame focuses your attention on a very specific aspect of the total picture, while a larger frame allows you to see the whole picture.

Have you ever been to a framing store? Most have adjustable frames that expand and contract, enabling you to see how your picture would look inside frames of various dimensions. How you frame your picture determines how viewers will interpret it because the frame you choose will highlight a specific aspect or portion of that picture. In fact, how you frame the picture determines the story it tells. Make the frame small and you narrow your perspective, yielding a certain kind of story. Enlarge the frame and you get a bigger perspective that invites a much different story. It's all a matter of perspective.

Since we're talking about actual pictures, let me show you a series of three scenes to help you grasp what I mean.

Do you see how the size of the frame shapes your perspective? The story changes each time the frame is enlarged. The same is true for how we frame our lives. The largest frame gives the most accurate and therefore the best perspective on our circumstances and past experiences. Most of us use too small a frame. We focus on a single, hurtful event and, based on that narrow perspective, make generalizations about everything else. We never see the big picture. Our lives revolve around a very limited part of the total picture, and we miss a larger, more meaningful perspective of life.

Forgiveness, however, allows you to change the story of your life by reframing your picture of your past. With empathy helping you understand the hurtful event from the other person's perspective and with humility helping you acknowledge that you have made similar mistakes, you will begin to see your story in a different light. By reframing your story, you change your memory of the past and so free yourself from its chains.

As I continue with our metaphor, realize that a grievance story frames the hurtful event with the smallest frame possible. A grievance story looks only at life's pain-filled moments and uses them, exclusively, to determine "what really happened." As you've recalled your grievance story, you've ignored items that didn't fit into your chosen frame of reference, and you've highlighted those experiences that did. In this way you created and framed a picture for the living room of your mind that you can gaze upon for the rest of your life—but it is not a pretty picture.

The process of reframing your story takes this very narrow perspective and begins to enlarge it, thus bringing about a broader and more accurate picture of your past. And the new story that emerges paves the way for your healing.

THE ADVANTAGE OF A LARGE FRAME

If your frame is so small that only life's bad stuff appears within it, you will then perceive that your whole life is miserable and ruined and that you can do nothing about it.

But if your frame is bigger and something bad takes place in one corner of the picture, you have a much larger context in which to place that hurtful event. Then you see it for what it really is: one bad thing surrounded by many good things. The larger your perspective, the less influence any single event can have over your life.

This framing process determines the context of your life experiences, and the larger the context, the more accurate the perspective you will have to help you forgive and heal. A large frame usually includes many experiences that can help balance your perspective on your life. For example, while all may seem hopeless now, a big frame reminds you that you have felt this way before and that you were able to come through it. Chances are you will come through it this time too. Having this larger picture available can encourage you in the tough times.

Imagine, for instance, that your best friend says something hurtful about you to someone else. If you focus only on that one conversation—if you give the event a very small frame—you are only able to view your friend in that hurtful context. Then you can't help but see your former friend as an enemy, for only an enemy would say such a terrible thing.

A larger frame, however, would remind you that this person has been your friend for many years. What she recently said does not fit with everything she has said before. As you use this larger frame for the picture of your friendship, you remember many good things she has said about you. You see that this one event doesn't match other parts of the picture. And, having placed her remark in this larger context, you don't conclude that your friend has become your enemy. Instead, you ponder how to approach her in order to better understand what she said. *After all*, you think, *the statement must have some context that I have not yet seen.* Asking your friend for clarification can be much more productive than accusing her of being no friend at all.

Clearly, when you use a larger frame of reference for your picture of the past, you see the person who hurt you as both good and bad rather than as exclusively evil. Yes, what she did in that situation was bad, but even as you realize that, you also see some of the good things about her. If you frame the hurtful event with an even larger frame, you can begin to see her history. You start taking into consideration some of the circumstances that might have caused her to be the way she is and act the way she does.

So be open to discovering a new way to think about the person who has wronged you. What in his life could have caused him to act the way he does? Maybe he's a perfectionist. Perfectionists have a habit of being overly critical, and they tend to offend the people they criticize. But if you understand that this person is being critical to try to compensate for what is missing in his own life, such as never receiving recognition or praise for his efforts, you realize that his negative comments have little to do with your shortcomings and a lot to do with his inner sense of inadequacy. Only as you gain this perspective can you see some good in him and recognize what he is dealing with. The hurtful incident is not all about you.

HOW LARGE IS YOUR FRAME?

How large is your frame? Some people have an exceedingly small frame—and it's not hard to know who those folks are. Whenever you speak with them—and the topic of conversation doesn't matter—they eventually circle back to their same old story. Whatever topic you introduce, they'll figure out in a matter of moments how to return to their old nesting grounds. These people have a very small frame for their story of misery and woe.

Other people have a slightly larger frame. They can talk about ten different topics, but even so their side of the conversation always sounds the same.

Still others have an even larger frame. They can talk about both good things and bad things, and they use their larger frame to consciously try to put most everything that happens to them in their proper context. People who use this larger frame seem to get the most out of life.

Now let me change metaphors for a minute. When problems threaten to overwhelm me and I want a larger perspective on my life, I climb the highest mountain I can find. I sit alone on the summit and gaze across the valleys below. When I have that vantage point, the big issues that have felt so overwhelming to me no longer look so big. In fact, they can seem downright small from this vantage point. I quickly begin to realize that my concerns are not as big as a mountain; they're a lot more like a molehill. Our perspective really does frame our reality.

So how big is *your* view of the world? Can you see the hurtful events in your life within a larger frame of reference and thus put them in a more realistic perspective? Seeing things in a new and bigger way doesn't change what happened, but it does enable you to say, "I can make my life better by choosing to see the big picture. I don't have to remain stuck in a one-event story." There is much more to your life than any single scene, so enlarge the dimensions of the frame around your story so that you can become aware of other, more life-giving realities.

LET IT GO

No matter what has happened to you in the past, it has already happened; there is nothing you can do to change it. So don't waste your time and energy trying to change what cannot be changed. Instead, change what you *can* change. Specifically, change what you are telling yourself about what happened in the past. You *can* revise your old grievance story.

And, yes, it's hard to let go of grievances, anger, and your desire for other people to suffer for what they did to you. But you are choosing to let go for many good reasons that now make perfect sense to you, aren't you? You let go for your own health and well-being, first of all. You let go of past hurts because you're glad that at another time someone let you off the hook, and now you extend that courtesy to someone else. And you let go because you have a larger frame of reference for understanding the hurt and for seeing the bigger picture of your life.

Letting go of grievances, anger, and the desire that the other person suffer is letting go of your grievance story. After all, you've realized that the old story no longer makes sense. It's no longer accurate. It no longer describes the whole picture. It's a bad story.

But letting go isn't just dismissing the old story from your mind, hoping that it goes away or that you'll forget it. Letting go is releasing the old grievance story because it no longer reflects your reality. That story is gone, replaced by a more accurate and more reliable story, a story that frees you from the past and allows you to go on with your life. The old story is no longer helpful or even truthful, so there's no point in telling it to yourself. You see that it no longer fits into your life story. It doesn't work for you anymore; in fact it would be harmful to your well-being to go back to that old story. So you move on.

Since you're no longer telling yourself the old story, you're no longer trapped in its hurtful world. You're free. A new story has completely replaced the old story. What didn't change, of course, are the facts. They didn't go away. The event itself is still relevant. You haven't forgotten it. But the story has changed so much that the event now has a radically different impact on you. It no longer keeps you from moving on with your life toward bigger and better things. Put as simply as possible, your life changes for the better when you reframe your old grievance story.

STEPS TO CHANGING A MEMORY

Forgiving people for events in the past happens as you change your memory of the past. So let me summarize the six key steps to changing a memory.

1. *Focus on what is true about the event from both your point of view and the offender's perspective.*

Try to step into the person's place and look at the incident from that vantage point. Rarely is one party completely at fault and the other totally blameless. What true observations from the other person's point of view can you import into your picture of the past event?

2. *Develop empathy for the person who hurt you.*

Empathizing means attempting to understand what might have motivated the behavior that was so hurtful. Start by trying to see the other person as a real human being, not as a demon who is completely and irredeemably evil.

3. *Identify the wrongs you yourself have committed that need forgiving.*

All of us—and that includes you—need forgiveness. When you realize that you have done things that require forgiveness and that you have been forgiven, you should be much more open to forgiving the person who hurt you. This willingness reveals a degree of humility.

4. *Revise your story so that it more accurately reflects the point of view of the offender as well as the offended.*

Dissect your original grievance story. Identify the elements that depend on a small frame in order to make your story appear true. Then make your frame as large as you can and try to see the incident in question as just one small part of the total picture of your life. Remember that your goal is to make your story more comprehensive and therefore more accurate.

5. *Look ahead at your life goals and take steps toward achieving them.*

What kind of future do you want for yourself? What can you start doing today to move toward accomplishing your goals and realizing your dreams? What do you need to stop doing today that is preventing you from reaching to the stars? Simply put, do what works and stop doing what doesn't work.

6. *Realize that forgiveness takes time; forgiveness is almost never achieved in a single attempt.*

Like most skills in life, forgiveness takes practice—and practice takes time. Rarely can someone forgive so completely and comprehensively in a single instant that old, negative thoughts and feelings never reappear. It may take awhile to forgive a particular event. One of my own experiences might help you better understand this.

Remember the story I told you about losing my job? Well, four years later, one of the decision makers who had approved my dismissal accepted a position at the very organization where I was currently working. Instantly, old feelings of woundedness and pain came rushing over me. I thought I had forgiven the incident, but renewed feelings of resentment and disappointment came crashing back into my life. How could I have genuinely forgiven if I still felt this way? I realized that I had to go back over old terrain and reframe my story once more.

As I did so, I saw that I had erred in thinking that I had not forgiven and that all my previous work had gone out the window. Rather, the recent event had merely challenged my new story—and that challenge invited some revising on my part. But the foundation from which to deal with this new experience had been laid in my previous forgiving. I could build on that foundation; I did not need to start over again.

So I made an appointment to meet with this individual. I didn't go in to let him know that I'd forgiven him for the terrible thing he had done; such an approach could have created a disaster. Instead, I hoped to learn new facts that I could then incorporate into my revised story. As a result of that conversation, I learned details about my dismissal and the thought process behind it that I had never known or even suspected. Armed with that new information, I successfully reframed my picture one more time and moved on.

By the way, today this former traitor (that's what I once considered him!) is again a good friend. Forgiveness works!

Yes, forgiveness definitely takes practice. So why not start practicing today?

TAKE CONTROL OF YOUR FUTURE

If you really want to get beyond the wounds of yesterday that continue to hurt you today, you have to forgive. Forgiveness doesn't change the reality of the past, but it does have the power to change your memory of the past. When you reframe your grievance story, you take much of the sting out of your past and transfer control of your life back into your own hands.

What other force has the ability to keep the past from continuing to disrupt your present? I know of nothing that works better than forgiveness. And, amazingly, its power doesn't extend just to the past. As you will see in the next chapter, forgiveness can significantly improve the present as well.

ASSIGNMENT

1. Reframe the grievance story you previously wrote by placing yourself, instead of the person who offended you, in charge of the outcome of your story.

2. Now place your grievance story in a larger frame by including all the information about the other person that you have discovered since the injury. What inconsistencies in your picture do you see? How does your story change?

3. What did you learn from this hurtful incident, and what lesson can you take from it in order to find healing and growth?

NINE

FORGIVING AND FINDING PEACE IN THE PRESENT

You can observe a lot by just watching.

—Yogi Berra

Is your head too often crowded by concern about the future or regrets about the past? Do you have trouble remaining fully aware
of the present? Do you struggle to live in the moment?

Most of us expend far too much energy worrying about the future or regretting the past. When you learn to not be so preoccupied by such worries or regrets, you will have the energy you need
to deal with your problems in the present.

In fact, focusing on the present puts you in the only place where
you can take control of your life. For the truth is, you can only control what happens in the here and now. You can't change the past.
What is past is past, and the future is yet to come. So everything you
do can only be done in the present. That's why getting in the present is key to taking charge of your life. When you are in control, it
is easier to find peace and contentment. I also want to let you in on
a secret: it is easier to forgive when you are content and not upset.

So what can you do to cultivate contentment? Contentment blos-
soms when what you *have* (present) overshadows what you *lack*
(past) as well as what you *want* (future). Dissatisfaction fills your
mind when you're thinking about all the reasons for your discontent.

In this chapter, I want to help you learn to focus on something other than reasons for your unhappiness so that you can know peace and contentment in the present. After all, a peaceful, contented state of mind will give you a better vantage point from which to live life. And—without question—with your mind at peace, you'll find it easier to forgive.

A FEW MORE TOOLS

As you have already learned, most of your upsetting thoughts come from the past. Sometimes your thoughts of the past and the accompanying emotions can be so overwhelming they keep you from clearly thinking through your present situation. You can't change the past, so why spend your time there?

If you want to let go of those disturbing thoughts from the past and get your mind into the present—the only place where contentment is possible—the following ideas will help you.

First of all, remember the mind/body connection we investigated in chapter 4? You can bring a measure of peace to your troubled heart by intentionally connecting your mind with your body. Both of the following starting points can begin your journey to contentment.

From Thought to Physical Response

THOUGHT → FEELING → PHYSIOLOGICAL RESPONSE

OR

From Physical Change to Thought

PHYSIOLOGICAL CHANGE → FEELING → THOUGHT

I will illustrate both processes for you because they work equally well.

FROM THOUGHT TO PHYSIOLOGICAL RESPONSE

I'm sure you've experienced something like this before: "For the past two weeks, I've been working to reframe an old, hurtful story—and then something unexpected happened that turned my world upside down again, and just like that, all the intense emotions came roaring back. I can't seem to get the old story out of my mind, and I know it's making me angry. What should I do?"

First, realize that you don't have to keep thinking about that old story. Even if you are having trouble reframing the story right now, you can take it off the table, so to speak. How? Simply by changing your thoughts.

"Yeah, right," you say. No, I mean it! Think of your thoughts as television channels. At any given moment, hundreds of stations are beaming their programs into millions of households. Which one you watch depends on which one you tune in to. Your mind works the same way. You could be thinking about fifty different things at any one time. Whatever you are thinking about is what your mind has tuned in to. You hold the remote, so to speak. If you don't like the thoughts that are currently playing in your mind, change the channel. You can say, "I'm not going to think about this right now. I'm going to think about something else." It sounds too simple, but it really does work!

Most people, however, see themselves as passive recipients of old memories. They believe that, once a thought just happens to pop into their mind, they have no choice but to think about that thought. Or perhaps these people have tried to get unwanted thoughts out of their mind, but the stubborn thoughts just don't go away. Why not? Because to try to stop thinking about something is to think about it.

To help me prove my point, try this experiment. Picture in your mind a fresh-picked lemon. See the dimples in its yellow skin? Slice it and squeeze some juice into your mouth. Let it drop on your tongue and taste its tartness. Feel the saliva fill your mouth. You have to swallow, don't you? Sure you do—and the stronger the image of a lemon is in your mind, the more saliva your body will produce. Got the picture? Good!

Now stop thinking about the lemon. I told you to stop thinking of that lemon. You're still thinking about that lemon, aren't you? You see? The harder you try to stop thinking about the lemon, the more you think about that lemon.

I come from New England, where my favorite fruit—especially in the fall—is a crisp Vermont Gold apple. Nothing can compare to an apple fresh off the tree. As soon as you get past its unique gold and red skin, the apple becomes snowy white, and the sweet juice inside is just to die for. And there is nothing like the crunch of an apple picked right from the tree on a brisk autumn day.

Did you notice what just happened? For the last fifteen seconds, you weren't thinking about a lemon; you were focusing on the apple. Why? Because I changed your mental channel. Thinking about apples stopped your thoughts about lemons. It really is possible, as we just demonstrated, to choose your thoughts. And by choosing your thoughts, you can also choose your emotional response because feeling follows thought.

This lemon-to-apple experiment illustrates the point that if you don't like what is currently playing in your mind—if it makes you angry and bitter—then change the channel. It's just like using the remote control of your TV: you can change the channel in your mind any time you choose.

MIND SURFING AND NEGATIVE THINKING

In my workshop on forgiveness, I give everyone a little plastic clicker and teach them a technique I call "mind surfing." It's kind of like channel surfing with a TV remote control except you're changing channels in your mind. I have participants carry the clicker around in their pocket. It actually makes a sound like the old kind of channel changer. I say, "Every time you're thinking about something you don't want to think about, reach into your pocket, click the clicker, go to another channel, and think about something else." Keep surfing the channels until you come to one you like. People who practice this technique have learned to change their thoughts any time they want to by simply choosing to think about something else.

But what do you do when your mind drifts back to the earlier thought? Just change the channel again. One effective way to do this is to think of your favorite place and, when you need to, go there in your mind. Yep, click over to the Travel Channel!

I travel a lot, and whenever I turn on the TV in my hotel room, it automatically goes to the hotel's default channel. That's usually not the channel I want to watch, but if I don't change it, that's the channel I will be watching. Now how smart would it be to watch that channel all night hoping something better will come on?

What is the default channel in your mind? What channel does your mind easily drift to throughout the day? What thoughts consume big chunks of your time, often in very unproductive ways? Remember, you just proved to yourself that you don't have to think about something simply because it pops into your mind. You can change the channel any time you choose and thereby change your thoughts and emotions.

(Just a word of caution here: to overuse this technique can be a form of denial and an unhealthy way of avoiding problems. I am not suggesting that you use this technique to avoid your problems. I'm just suggesting that if you would prefer not to think about something at this moment, change the thought and come back to it later.)

Now let's get back to the mind/body connection. Once you change your thought, what happens to your feelings? They also change. So if you're thinking about that miserable, no-good jerk who hurt you, your feelings grow from that unpleasant thought. But if instead you wonder, *What am I going to make for dinner to-night?* your thoughts change to hunger, and all of a sudden your body is producing saliva and gastric juices. Your feelings change as your thoughts do. The more stressful the thoughts, the more tense your body becomes. Conversely, the more peaceful your thoughts, the more relaxed your body.

So, once more, the first pathway looks like this:

THOUGHT → FEELING → PHYSIOLOGICAL RESPONSE

Your feelings do not have to rule you because you can choose to change your thoughts and, consequently, change your feelings. If you're still not convinced, think about what sailors do. They don't control the wind, but they learn how to work with it to reach their destination. Likewise, rather than trying to control the emotional winds swirling around you, set your sails for the direction you would like to go and then head that way. It is much better to set your course than be buffeted here and there by contrary winds of emotion.

Again, you can change what you feel and therefore how your body reacts by choosing to think about something else. And this process works just as well from the other direction.

From Physiological Change to Thought

Once again ugly thoughts of this no-good jerk have popped into your mind, and you can't stop thinking about him. Your body is tense and you feel totally stressed. What can you do?

You could choose this second pathway to peace. You could concentrate on relaxing your body, an act that will change your emotions, which will, in turn, make it much easier for you to think about something more pleasant and peaceful. The simplest way to relax is to take slow, deep breaths. It's a technique called diaphragmatic breathing.

Take a Breath Break

People take many kinds of breaks—coffee breaks, smoking breaks, lunch breaks, chocolate breaks—during the day. Well, I'd like you to take a breath break. I know you're already breathing, but I'd like you to think about it. Here are the steps to follow:

1. Get in a comfortable position either sitting in a chair or lying on the floor. Be careful not to slouch because that can restrict

your breathing. Don't be stiff, but keep your spine as straight as you comfortably can.

2. As you slowly inhale, think of your belly as a balloon that you are blowing up. Place your hands on your belly as it expands and contracts. Watch your hands rise as you inhale and fall each time you exhale.

3. Fill your lungs and then empty them completely. You may want to push gently on your belly each time you exhale to ensure that you are emptying your lungs.

4. Breathe slowly. For a good pace, slowly count to five as you inhale; then count to five as you exhale. Pause briefly in the moment between exhaling and inhaling.

5. Breathe in through your nose and out through your mouth. Doing so allows a slight cooling of the nasal passage that can actually cool your brain. A cool thinker really does make better decisions than a hothead, so chill.

As you slowly inhale and exhale, your heart rate and blood pressure will start to go down. As you slow down, your tensed muscles will also start to relax. They do so because you are soothing every muscle in your body with rich, oxygenated blood, enabling them to relax and rebuild.

This form of breathing is the starting point for many spiritual and religious practices, such as meditation, prayer, and yoga. It is probably no happenstance that, in many world languages, the word for spirit is the same word that is used for breath.

- *Ruach* is Hebrew for both spirit and breath.

- *Pneuma* is Greek for both spirit and breath.

- *Spiritus* is Latin for both spirit and breath.

- *Chi* is Japanese for both spirit and breath.

Now back to the breathing exercise. While you breathe slowly, pay attention to the moment. If any thoughts come into your mind, don't engage them; simply notice them and let them go. Concentrate on your breathing in order to stay focused on the here and now. The goal of this exercise is to:

- Relax your body

- Quiet your mind

- Place yourself in the here and now

Many people will find it difficult to do this exercise. They have a hard time sitting still and doing nothing. If this describes you and you would prefer to be doing something as you relax, let me suggest another exercise.

PROGRESSIVE MUSCLE RELAXATION

The following technique, called progressive muscle relaxation, gets your body more involved in the process while you practice slow, deep breathing. Here are the steps of progressive relaxation:

1. Begin with the breathing exercise described above.

2. Every time you inhale, tighten a muscle group. Every time you exhale, release and relax the muscles you just tightened. Let your muscles go totally limp and pause for a second or two before inhaling again. I suggest moving through the muscle groups in the following order:
   - Your toes
   - The arches in your feet
   - Your calf muscles
   - Your hips
   - Your buttocks
   - Your stomach
   - Your chest
   - Your hands (make a fist)
   - Your forearms

- Your biceps
- Your shoulders
- Your neck
- Your jaw and your temples

3. Tighten and relax each muscle group three times before moving on to the next.

4. If you notice particular tension in any muscle group, tighten and relax those muscles five times.

As you do this exercise, you're letting go not only of your stress, but also of the high-energy emotions that cause your stress. You simply cannot sustain intense thoughts or feelings when you're physically relaxed. This is the second pathway of the body to the mind, and it is illustrated below.

PHYSIOLOGICAL CHANGE → FEELING → THOUGHT

Unfortunately, relaxation and stillness of soul are not popular in our day. In fact, most people consider being still a colossal waste of time. Furthermore, we fill our lives with noise—and the marketers of the world contribute to that with annoying phone calls, the barrage of billboards along the highway, louder-than-the-TV-program commercials, and the relentless spam messages that come into your computer mailbox. So, I challenge you to be countercultural and to experience for yourself the value of relaxation and quiet.

If you're still not convinced of the value of stillness, consider that all of life consists of cycles of stress and recovery. Tension depletes energy, but relaxation releases tension and gives you more energy to invest in life. Life then brings more stress and tension, and the cycle continues. People who live with constant stress are not able to benefit from the rebuilding of the nerves and muscles that happens during the recovery cycle because they never seem able to relax. We refer to that experience over time as burnout. If that's you, be warned!

Now that you've read about the breathing exercise and the muscle-relaxation exercise, let me reassure you that you don't need to carve out one-hour blocks of time in order to benefit from either of them. You need only three to five minutes, four to six times a day, to take a few deep breaths and think about something peaceful and relaxing. Your body and nerves will thank you by being stronger and steadier and ready for action when you are.

Also, remember that, by doing these exercises, you can intervene at either the intellectual or physical level and change any hurtful emotions you may be dealing with right now. Rather than feeling all upset, you can be more at peace by changing your thoughts or by relaxing your body. With practice, you will become proficient at calming your body and quieting your mind.

A Few More Tools

So far I've asked you to focus on controlling your internal environment: your thoughts, your feelings, and your body's response to stress. But your external environment—light, sounds, colors, and smells—also influences you, creating either more stress for you or making it easier for you to relax. Your external environment can greatly impact your internal being. So let me describe these four external stimuli that have a profound ability either to help you relax and be at peace or to keep you distressed and depressed.

The Role of Light

Many compelling studies indicate that light deprivation leads to an increase in depression. Supporting that conclusion is the fact that depression tends to become more prevalent during the winter months when sunlight hours dwindle.

So don't deprive yourself of the sun and its healing and regenerative powers. When dark thoughts of past hurts begin to pummel you, try going out for a walk and basking in the sunshine. Whatever you do, don't hide away in a gloomy room with only your unpleasant thoughts.

If you live in an area where cloudy days seem to stretch into dark weeks and depressing months, you may have to get a bit more creative than simply stepping outside. Look into buying some full-spectrum light fixtures that imitate the healthful light of the sun. Or try to schedule shorter, more frequent vacations to places that offer more sunshine. Whatever it takes to bathe yourself in more light, do it.

The Impact of Color

Some colors are peaceful and relaxing, while others are much more intense. Earth-tone colors—yellows, beiges, and lighter hues—tend to help you relax. Homes decorated in such muted colors make it easier for most people to remain calm. Homes in purples, oranges, and other bright, intense colors tend to create a more stressful environment. These more vibrant colors may be good for the playroom, but they are not as helpful in your quiet room.

The Effect of Aromas

To this day the smell of freshly baked bread takes me back to the small bakery down the block from my childhood home. The memory creates such a positive feeling that I sometimes intentionally drive by a bakery just to revisit that feeling.

I also love the smell of castor oil—blended with motor oil—being burned by a race car revving its engine to the highest RPMs. I recognize that distinctive smell every time I'm near a racetrack, and it makes me feel as if I could go out there on the track and mix it up with the best of them.

On the other hand, I have a distinctly negative reaction to the smell of cheese. Not just any cheese, but Limburger cheese. My grandparents savored that taste, but the smell always repulsed me, a reaction that lingers to this day.

Yes, smells can have a very powerful effect over us, helping us feel peaceful and calm or irritated and jumpy. For instance, scents associated with natural things—flowers, fresh air, the sea—tend to have a soothing effect on most people because those aromas take them, in their minds, to a garden, a mountain retreat, or a beautiful beach. But smells can also have exactly the opposite effect. For example, if your dentist has lilacs in her office, what might be a pleasant smell for some could trigger a negative response for you. Only you know which aromas will help you create a more soothing environment.

The Power of Sound

Sound may be the most significant environmental factor influencing your level of stress and your ability to relax. If someone outside your window goes at a jackhammer all day long, what does that do to your nerves? Unless you're deaf, it will unravel them—and even if you can't hear, the constant vibrations may still drive you crazy.

One of the most effective ways to control the noise in your environment is through the use of music. With music, you control the volume, the beat, the intensity, the tone, and the range. Consider, for instance, how the crescendos in classical music raise the intensity and cause you to feel the stress as the volume builds—and, in sharp contrast, how the diminuendos slow you down and relax you.

Recently, some musicians have dedicated their talents to producing what they call "healing sound tracks" that are designed to encourage calm and peace in the listener. These tracks might employ sounds from nature, such as waterfalls or babbling brooks, the haunting calls of animals, the song of a bird, or the crackling of a fire. The goal of this type of music is to gently bring the audience to a calmer, more soothing, and more restful place. If you've ever visited a massage therapist, you probably listened to a healing sound track as you relaxed on the table.

Heavy-metal music, on the other hand, has a strong, rhythmic beat that brings dissonance into its cacophony of sound. Its lyrics often scream out all that's wrong with the world and encourage opposition to—and even violence against—those problems. It's even been suggested that, before some people commit a crime, they crank up the music to give themselves the kind of frenetic energy they want.

You'll hear a different kind of music at sporting events, though. There the driving sound gets the crowd cheering and the players moving. When management wants to energize the team and its fans, it plays certain songs to get everyone pumped up—songs like "We Will Rock You" or "Who Let the Dogs Out."

As these examples suggest, music tends to bypass the cognitive and go directly to the emotional. So what kind of music might help you find a measure of peace? Since musical taste is highly personal, it's hard for someone else to predict what will work best for you. So feel free to play any music you find relaxing. I can safely say that music with a heavy beat and major dissonance is going to lead to more tension and that music featuring more melody and softer tones usually leads to calmness, but I can't say much more than that. Bottom line, you have to figure out what particular kind of music works best for you.

All of these environmental factors—light, color, aromas, and sound—can have a significant impact on your ability to relax your body and slow down your thoughts. I encourage you to choose wisely so that you will experience the kind of peace that allows you to complete the difficult, but rewarding, work of forgiveness.

LIVE TODAY

Do you fully understand that this moment is all you have? We can only live in the present, but far too many people make the mistake of trying to live either in the past or in the future. Again, the only time we are ever alive is *now*. And if you are not living in the now, you are not living. To *not* be present in the moment is to lose that moment in time forever. So do what you must to find peace in the present—and don't forget to enjoy yourself! As that familiar expression reminds us, "Take time to smell the roses." After all, you will never have this moment again.

Of course, if you play it right, these wonderful, smell-the-roses moments can stretch into a lovely future and across your entire lifetime. And—do I need to say it?—forgiveness can lead you there.

After all, the focus of this book is forgiveness, and before you extend any words of forgiveness to anybody, let me encourage you to take some time to relax and get in the right frame of mind. Carefully think through both *what* you will say and *how* you will say it. Don't rush this planning phase. Be thoughtful and reflective. This could be a defining moment in your life, so don't hurry it.

I have also found that it is easier to forgive when you are relaxed and at peace than when you are angry and all upset. So chill, relax, and quiet down. You will then find forgiveness an easier thing to do.

Of course learning to relax is not the same as forgiving, but it does create a better place from which to forgive. It's simply easier to forgive when you're calm than when you're tense and upset. If you take the time to get into the right frame of mind, your thoughts will slow down, your emotions will cool, and you'll be better able to step back, take in the larger picture, and evaluate your choices. Your mind will no longer be racing around or focusing on a single story to the point that you're obsessing about it. So take a breath, lean back, and forgive.

By doing this, you stop your automatic reaction to whoever hurt or offended you. You seize that moment between stimulus and response to truly reflect and make a wise choice. If you're in a relaxed frame of mind, you are more likely to consider forgiveness an option. In this place of contentment, you will make the best choice for your future.

It makes sense, doesn't it, that forgiveness is most likely to occur when you are in your place of peace and contentment, so practice getting there today.

ASSIGNMENT

1. Take time today to practice the relaxation breathing technique you read about. Follow these simple steps to enter a place of peace.

   a. Either sit up straight in a chair or lie on your back. Make sure to keep your spine straight even after you find a comfortable position. (Modification is allowed!)

   b. Close your eyes.

   c. Breathe in through your nose and out through your mouth.

   d. Watch your belly rise and fall.

   e. Breathe slowly.

   f. Focus on your exhaling . . . and your inhaling. . . . If a thought enters your mind, notice it and then let it go. This practice in letting go of an undesired thought will help you let go when it's time to forgive those who have hurt you.

2. Now that you're in this more relaxed place, I want you to imagine forgiving a person who has hurt you. Identify the advantages of forgiving while you're at peace like this rather than when you are upset.

TEN

FORGIVING AND FINDING HOPE FOR THE FUTURE

Nobody can go back and start a new beginning,
but anyone can start today and make a new ending.
— Maria Robinson

here can be no future without forgiveness."
So spoke Desmond Tutu, the first black archbishop of Capetown and recipient of the Nobel Peace Prize. He came to this conclusion after serving as chairman of the Truth and Reconciliation Commission, a group formed to look into gross human-rights violations committed during South Africa's shameful era of apartheid.

South Africa was deeply divided by racism, and when blacks finally won the right to vote in 1993, most observers expected widespread bloodletting to follow. They foresaw an epidemic of murderous vendettas, large-scale riots, cities in flames, uncontrolled brutality, and mayhem everywhere. *How could it be otherwise?* they wondered. After all, the white minority had oppressed the black majority for decades. Millions of people lived with revenge on their minds, and outsiders thought that these former enemies would surely destroy each other. How could such a nation have any kind of future at all?

Desmond Tutu answered the question with a single word: forgiveness. Only through forgiveness could the people of South Africa hope for a viable future for their reborn nation. Tutu knew that the ability to forgive is essential to being a part of a healthy community because only forgiveness enables imperfect people to live together in peace.

Forgiveness says, "We are going to move from what was toward what can be." Forgiveness allows the wounded to let go of their yesterdays in order to build their tomorrows. With forgiveness, there is a future for all of us.

THE LINK BETWEEN FORGIVENESS AND HOPE

Forgiveness and hope are inseparably linked. In fact, forgiveness gives birth to hope because forgiveness insists that, in the end, it is better to move toward your desired future than to live chained to your unwanted past. That is why you forgive. You don't need to even the score; you simply need to go on with your life. Forgiveness helps you let go of the pain from your past and embrace hope for your future.

Forgiveness also leads to a reorganization of thoughts and a reconstruction of dreams. Forgiveness has the ability to release you from the hurts of your past so you can energetically pursue your future. Forgiveness makes a fresh start in life possible.

Just as your grievance story kept you trapped in the past, it also shapes and defines your future. And that's exactly what your grievance story is doing if you find yourself thinking, *Life is bad now, and it's going to be worse tomorrow.*

Forgiveness changes all this. When you revise your grievance story by incorporating a bigger-picture perspective, your past no longer keeps you trapped. But forgiveness doesn't stop at helping you let go of the past. Forgiveness also has the ability to shape your future. Built right into forgiveness is a driving optimism about the future.

Do you see how hope and forgiveness fuel each other? If I have no hope, why should I forgive? And why would I forgive if not for the possibility of gaining something better—and that's what hope is all about. Forgiveness and hope march together, arm in arm, in the same parade. When you choose to forgive, you link up with hope and therefore find your way to a brighter future.

"If Only . . ." vs. "What If . . . ?"

Psychologists tell us there are two kinds of people in this world: optimists and pessimists. The pessimist sees the doughnut hole, while the optimist sees the doughnut. The pessimist sees the glass half empty; the optimist sees the glass half full. The pessimist says, "Because of all the miserable stuff from my past, my life can only get worse." The optimist says, "All these terrible things from the past have given me the opportunity to learn and grow so that I'm stronger for the challenges that lie ahead."

Forgiveness has the power to turn pessimists into optimists. It helps the forgiver see the world differently and gain a new perspective on life. Circumstances, relationships, jobs—any and every aspect of life really can get better. And that's what I mean by applying forgiveness to the future. Forgiveness is letting go of the past and taking hold of the future.

Too many of us, however, spend big chunks of time thinking *if only* . . . rather than *what if* . . . ? The pessimistic "if only" reveals a desire to go back and change the past even though the past is finished and can't be changed. You can hear that in statements like "If only I had said no when he first asked me out on a date" and "If only I had studied more in school."

On the other hand, optimistic "what if" thinking looks to the future, sets some clearly defined goals, and then prioritizes activities in order to achieve those goals. "What if" thinking focuses on possibilities rather than impossibilities: "What if I got that scholarship, went back to school, and completed my degree?" or "What if I tried that new business venture and it actually worked?"

Which kind of thinker are you? Has forgiveness begun to free you from the "if onlys" so that you can pursue the "what ifs"?

You see, over time, your outer world becomes a reflection of your inner world. In other words, you become what you spend the majority of your time thinking about. Successful people, for instance, think about what they want and how to get it. Unsuccessful people think about what they don't have and spend their time either wishing life were different or wondering whom they can blame for their current situation. They complain rather than achieve.

Think for a moment about your own future. Do you know where you're going? Do you have a clear idea of what you'd like to see happen in your life? Have you determined your purpose in life? What do you hope to accomplish during your years on this planet? People with a clearly understood purpose and a well-defined mission in life know where they are going, and they are determined to get there.

So, if forgiveness has begun its work of freeing you from your painful past, let's consider the next steps you can take in order to achieve your desired goals.

GOALS: RUNGS ON THE LADDER TO SUCCESS

You may have heard it said, "Some people spend their whole lives climbing the corporate ladder only to find it resting against the wrong wall." That image is a powerful reminder that success in the world's eyes does not necessarily lead to your personal satisfaction. What *do* you want out of life?

The goals you choose for your life will both define and unlock your future. If you have no specific goals, it doesn't matter what you do; your activities are somewhat pointless. After all, you have very little chance of hitting a target you cannot clearly identify, especially when you have no idea where the target should be. But if you have specific goals and live with them firmly in your mind, then everything you do should move you one step closer to fulfilling them and achieving your desired future.

But how important is goal setting to you? My dad used to say, "If wishes were horses, then beggars would ride." When I would dream rather than act, my father used this statement to ask me the same question I want to ask you: are you willing to make sacrifices now in order to achieve your goals tomorrow? In other words, are your goals for the future important enough to you to motivate you to do something about reaching them today?

If all this talk of goals makes sense to you, then you're in the last phase of the forgiveness process: you're moving away from the past and toward the future you desire.

THE BASICS OF EFFECTIVE GOAL SETTING

Stop and look around. Everything you see began as an idea that someone believed could become a reality. These determined doers lived the maxim "What you can conceive, you can achieve."

So, if you have goals but aren't achieving them, then you need to learn the skills that people who *are* reaching their goals have mastered. It isn't easy to achieve goals, but fulfilling them is definitely worth your effort. So are you ready, through forgiveness, to let go of the past and embrace your future by setting goals and then working toward them?

Wait, you say. Not so fast. I've set goals for my life in the past only to have someone get in my way. I'm not so sure I want to be disappointed again. It hurts too much to try and fail. This kind of thinking can sabotage a good idea before you even get started. So choose a mindset of determination and don't give up despite the naysayers in your life.

After all, you are putting yourself on a different path when you choose to forgive. On this path you leave behind your painful past. You also act on the realization that no one but you is responsible for your life. So you take charge. You let your dreams, not your past, guide you. And you set specific goals in order to achieve those dreams.

As you set these goals that will help guide your journey, understand that all attainable goals have at least five things in common. Your goals should be:

1. Written

Take the time and make the effort to put your goals in writing. Goals become real only when you write them down. In hospital work we have a saying: "If it wasn't written, it didn't happen." So put your goals in writing if you want them to happen. Once you've written down your goals, you own them; they're yours. If you don't put your goals in writing, they will remain vague wishes of what might be ("Well, maybe this is what I'll do. I just don't know for sure."). Don't let that happen to you! Get out some paper, write down your goals, and say, "That's where I'm going." Once you've put your goals on paper, you're on your way to achieving them.

2. Specific

The clearer the goal, the easier it is to determine exactly what you need to do to get there. Let's say your goal is to be happy. While happiness is something all of us desire, what exactly would happiness entail for you—and what will you do to get there? A clearer goal might be to learn to play the guitar. You may have always enjoyed music, especially sitting around the campfire and singing familiar tunes that warm your heart. Learning to play the guitar is a clear goal, and your happiness would be a consequence of achieving that goal.

3. Sequenced

Once you have a clear goal, ask yourself what specific steps will get you there and in what sequence you will need to take those steps. In the example above, for instance, you would need to purchase a guitar and take some music lessons. But before you buy just any guitar, you need to know what type of music you would like to play. Do you need an electric or an acoustic guitar to play the kind of music you enjoy? Next, you need to ask around to find a good music teacher. Then you'll need to decide whether you'll take lessons once a week or twice a week. That will depend, at least in part, on how much practice time you can carve out each day. By the way, when will you practice and for how long? This kind of thinking leads to success because the more specifically you define each step you need to take to achieve your goals, the easier it will be for you to reach those goals.

4. Measurable

Make sure that progress toward your goals can be measured and then find a practical way to track that progress. In the case of guitar lessons, you could measure your progress by taping your practice sessions once a month. Then you could go back and listen to the tapes to hear how you've improved. Another way to measure improvement might be to track your progress through a lesson book. You know that the music becomes more technical and complex with each succeeding lesson. So mastery of each lesson means progress toward your guitar-playing goal.

Measurable goals allow you to track your progress over time. They can encourage you to persevere. Success, in turn, helps fuel continued effort. Each step you take in the right direction motivates you to continue the journey.

5. Scheduled

Establishing a schedule for each step allows you to see whether you're making progress at a pace that will allow you to achieve your goals within the time you have set for yourself. An example of a time-based goal might be something like "I want to finish preparing the baby's room one month before my wife's due date." Along the way, you can adjust the time frames you set to make sure they remain both reasonable and achievable.

After you have developed your goals and made sure that they meet these five criteria, step back and let them sit for a few days. During that time, read through them several times and ask yourself, "Do these goals really reflect my life's priorities? Will my goals help me fulfill my life's purpose? Can I get excited about spending my time working toward these goals?" If the answer to these questions is yes, then you are definitely on the right track.

THREE KINDS OF GOALS

As you've probably noticed, I like to think of life as a journey. If you are heading in the right direction and are making steady progress, then you will eventually arrive at your chosen destination. But when you put too much emphasis on results, you can place too much pressure on yourself, and that can actually discourage progress. You don't need that kind of pressure—and you know what I'm talking about if you ever lived with a well-intentioned but overbearing parent who always asked, "Is that the best you can do?" or "Have you finished yet?" That kind of pressure just isn't helpful.

So learn what I learned the hard way when I started an exercise program on my fiftieth birthday. I had been gaining some weight and was clearly not as fit as I had been when I was younger. I also wanted to somehow slow down this aging thing. So, having exercised very little in the months leading up to my big 5-0, I went out and ran five miles. While I was a little sore that day—or so I convinced myself that's all it was—the next morning I was in pure agony. I could hardly walk, let alone run. I learned that I needed to take smaller steps (or at least fewer of them) in order to achieve my goal.

Learn from my mistake and know that your ability to achieve your goals is all but guaranteed if you enjoy the journey and take small steps toward those goals each and every day. You may not feel as if you're making progress, but if you are taking consistent steps toward your goals each day, you will get closer and closer to achieving your goals with each passing week. Success really is achieved one step at a time.

But obviously there is more than one step in the journey. So, as you plan your trip, you may find it helpful to think of your goals as short-term, intermediate, and long-term. Each of these three types serves a different purpose, but they all work together toward the same ultimate end: getting you where you want to be.

1. Short-term goals

Short-term goals are the initial tasks you need to do today to start your journey. They define specific action steps that are immediately doable. Short-term goals focus on what you can work on today or this week to move toward your desired future.

A goal that could be realized in the short-term might be to plan a vacation to a favorite destination. That vacation could be an important step toward your longer-term goal of living a more balanced life. Or if you've always wanted to work with flowers but never thought you could, a short-term goal might be to volunteer to work in a florist shop for an hour or so a week. Or maybe you'd like to find a new career. You're thinking, *I've stayed with this job because I felt it was the only thing I could do. I never went to college because my spouse left me and I couldn't afford it. I had to raise the children, so I didn't have time to get the skills I needed.* A good short-term goal might be to research a different field of work or take a night class that would enable you to explore new options.

With practice, you will get good at setting and achieving short-term goals. The process will become a regular part of the way you approach life, and these short-term goals will help guide your daily decisions. Once you are comfortable with this goal-setting skill, it's time to aim higher.

2. Intermediate goals

In what ways would you like your life to be different a year from now? Do you want to meet a new friend? Start a new business? Get to know other people in your neighborhood? What do you want to accomplish in the next twenty-four months?

Intermediate goals will take you between a month and several years to achieve. For example, obtaining an academic degree is an intermediate goal. You achieve intermediate goals only as a result of successfully completing a series of short-term goals. In this case, going to school each week is a short-term goal. Completing your course work and graduating is an intermediate goal. Clearly, intermediate goals are not immediate goals—they cannot be achieved right away—but they are possible to reach as you take appropriate steps each day.

3. Long-term goals

Long-term goals keep you inspired, fuel your passion, and strengthen your resolve. They set a worthy target some distance out into the future. In our illustration above, a long-term goal would be a new career, one that is satisfying and rewarding. To reach this major life goal, you first have to complete your short-term as well as your intermediate goals.

Those dreams for tomorrow—those long-term goals—both arise from and contribute to your ultimate meaning and purpose in life. To determine your long-term goals, therefore, you should first ask yourself these questions: When you're lying on your deathbed, what will you wish you had done? What did you really want to accomplish in your life? Did you want to be a good parent to your children? Did you want to help people in the third world? Again, your long-term goals ultimately define who you are as a person as well as what you will become.

Now write down your own long-term goals and start figuring out what you need to do *today* to get moving in that direction. What must you do this year? What will you need to be doing two years from now? Each day aim to do one thing that will take you another step closer to fulfilling your goals. After all, each step you take moves you one step closer to achieving your dreams.

KEEP THE MAIN THING THE MAIN THING

To achieve your goals, you must take care to keep the main thing the main thing. Reaching your goals is all about living life according to your priorities; it's about not letting urgent matters crowd out the important things.

In my forgiveness workshop I make this point with the following object lesson. I hold up a container filled to the top with large plastic blocks. I then ask, "Is the container full?" People say yes, but then I add some sand to the container, thus filling up the spaces between the blocks. Then I ask again, "Is the container full now?" It looks like it, but then I add a quart of water to the container—and every drop fits.

What would happen, however, if I first filled the container with water? Would there be enough room left for the sand or the blocks? No way.

And that is precisely my point. "If you first get the big things, the truly important things, in place in your life," I explain, "there will always be room for the other things. But if you first try to get all the little things done, there will never be room for the larger, more important things."

So be sure that you're making progress every day on the most important goals in your life. Prioritize your most crucial activities. Keep the main thing the main thing. If you do, you can be pretty sure that the smaller things will also find room. And if they don't all fit in, so what? Better to miss a small thing or two along the way than to not have room for the big things that are really important to you.

THREE BARRIERS TO OVERCOME

Most, if not all, of us can agree that setting goals for ourselves is key to having the kind of life we want. So why doesn't everybody do this? I've identified three main reasons why some folks don't set goals for themselves:

1. People fail to fully realize the importance of setting goals.

If you grew up in an environment where goal setting was not done, you may not realize how important goals really are. So let me say again that goals make it possible for you to accomplish what you want to in life. Without goals—without clear targets to shoot at—you can waste a lot of time and energy going nowhere. Setting goals and working toward them enables you to establish and enjoy the future you desire.

If your dreams never seem to come true, perhaps it's because you have never translated them into clear, attainable goals. Dreams tend to stay dreams until solid goals help them move from the realm of fantasy to the kingdom of reality.

2. People don't know how to set goals.

For starters, maybe you never knew what a real goal was. Maybe you never understood how goal setting can help you reach the future you want for yourself.

Many people, however, mistake wishes for goals, but the two are very different. Goals identify specific action steps necessary for achieving the goal; they focus on the process. Wishes merely look to the end point; they offer very few specific steps for getting there.

Maybe you—like many others—never grasped that functional goals need to be written down in clear, specific, and measurable ways. Or maybe you never saw the difference between a short-term goal, an intermediate goal, and a long-term goal.

But now you know. And now you need to get busy setting your goals.

3. People fear failure.

Most successful people will tell you that for every success they enjoyed, they endured many more failures. Failed efforts don't mean you are a failure; rather, they show that you are working toward success. Learning from your failures will make you smarter than most of the people you'll ever meet. Success is all about taking risks.

Remember the first time you fell off your bike when you were learning to ride it? Falling was not failing; we all take tumbles when we learn a new skill. Not getting back up on the bike and trying again—*that* would be failing. But in your case, because you wanted to take off down the block—that was your goal—you picked yourself up and tried again and again. Before you knew it, you could ride around the block—and you've been able to ride a bike ever since.

Success comes not by avoiding risks, but by risking failure.

TIME TO MOVE ON

As Desmond Tutu observed, there really is no future without forgiveness. That old grievance story of yours would gladly keep you chained to the past. But forgiveness allows you to let go of the past, to live in the present, and to look forward to the new possibilities your future holds.

As forgiveness frees you from your hurtful past, it also gives you the opportunity to shape your future. In other words, forgiveness offers you hope regardless of where you have come from, what you have done, or what's been done to you. Your past does not matter; what does matter is your future. And, with forgiveness, you really do get two for the price of one: release from your past as well as hope for your future.

ASSIGNMENT

1. List your major life goals as specifically as you can. If this is difficult for you, don't be discouraged. Know that many people struggle with this. Also, remember that developing goals is like any skill in life: you will get better with practice.

2. Next, break down your goals into short-term, intermediate, and long-term action steps.

3. Now ask yourself what you need to do *today* to take one step toward achieving your goals—and do it!

ELEVEN

A FEW CAUTIONS

Mistakes are a part of being human.
Appreciate your mistakes for what they are:
precious life lessons that can only be learned the hard way.
Unless it's a fatal mistake, which, at least, others can learn from.

—Al Franken

Forgiveness did not come easy for me. I made mistakes along the way that hindered my ability to forgive. At times I became discouraged and felt like giving up. So, hoping that you can learn from my mistakes, I want to share with you a few words of caution based on lessons I learned as I traveled my own journey to forgiveness.

1. *When forgiveness is offered too quickly, it may not be forgiveness*
   at all. It may just be avoidance.

Rather than facing their pain and dealing with it, some people try to escape it as quickly as possible. This sort of quick forgiveness isn't forgiveness at all. It allows people to hide their real pain, but it solves nothing. Don't confuse pretending the problem isn't there with the reality that the problem does exist and must be dealt with.

How many times have you seen people use this faulty strategy? A hurtful incident occurs, and the injured person says, "Oh, that's OK. I forgive you. Don't worry about it." When we offer forgiveness too quickly like this, we avoid the hard but necessary work of naming the problem, talking about the hurt it has caused, and seeking a mutually satisfying solution. Also, quick forgiveness does nothing to change a grievance story. In fact, it can keep you chained to your story because it closes the door to any future conversation about the incident since the incident has been quickly "forgiven" and dismissed. Again, quick forgiveness isn't forgiveness at all. It's an unhealthy strategy that basically seeks to hide the hurt, bury it, and forget it.

Sweeping the offense under the carpet isn't helpful when your goal is to reframe the past, not ignore it. Although it is initially stressful to confront a problem and truthfully share your perspective, doing so can be very rewarding for everyone involved. The problem is effectively dealt with and therefore less likely to reappear sometime later.

> *2. Forgiveness is not forgiveness when it's used as a tool of one-upmanship.*

Did you know that the words "I forgive you" can be a way for the offended party to elevate him- herself above the offender? Those three words can mean "I am better than you because of what you have done to me, and that self-appointed status will be my reward." In fact, some people actually look for faults in others in order to be able to say, "I forgive you." In this way they believe they elevate themselves over others. This is really nothing more than a clever way to turn the tables. So beware of forgiveness being used as a tool of one-upmanship. That form of forgiveness is merely about position, not authenticity.

> *3. Some people use forgiveness as a weapon of vengeance.*

Have people ever said, "I forgive you"—and you wish they hadn't? You really didn't want their forgiveness. It actually annoyed you. You thought, *Why are you forgiving me?* You felt as though the real motive behind that forgiveness was to set you up as the one who did wrong. This statement of forgiveness allowed the speaker to pose as a magnanimous, loving, and wonderful human being who could graciously forgive a vile sinner like you.

Real forgiveness should create equality, not inferiority. Forgiveness provides a stage on which two adults speak to each other in a mutually beneficial way. And forgiveness is a way of responding to wrongs done, not a tool to make others look wrong.

4. Avoid forgiveness that shuts you off from your feelings.

Superficial forgiveness not only shuts you off from your feelings, but, in effect, turns them off. And when you don't feel one emotion, you feel other emotions less strongly as well. Your feelings are interconnected; they are not isolated one from the other. Consider passion, for instance. It can be driven by love as well as anger, and often passion is a little of both. Cut yourself off from your anger, and your passion diminishes.

People who avoid their feelings also frequently avoid closeness, thus starting a cycle of withdrawal and isolation. This can lead to depression and a point where they no longer feel anything. But the goal of genuine forgiveness, of course, is not to become more detached from life but to become more invested in it.

5. Some so-called forgiveness softens the immediate conflict at the price of one's self-worth or well-being; the cost may even be revictimization.

Any offer of forgiveness that makes you feel small, powerless, or afraid is never worth giving. You may think you are reducing the problem by avoiding a big blowup, but when the underlying problems are not addressed, know that the trouble *will* come up again.

So be careful of any attempt at forgiveness that diminishes your self-worth. That's what is happening when thoughts like these pass through your mind: *I forgive you, but deep inside I believe you will do it again* or *I forgive you because I am so afraid that I can't stand up to you.* Forgiveness should always be an act of strength. You forgive because you desire—and, I would add, deserve—to be free of the past and to have a better future.

Never forgive from a position of weakness; that merely reinforces the offenders' belief that they can step all over you whenever they want to. A forgiver is not a doormat, and forgiveness does not say, "It's OK. Let's not talk about it." A forgiver is actually assertive and very clear about what's expected of the offender and what won't be tolerated: "What was done in the past is unacceptable, and it simply must not happen again. If it does, there will be consequences." Such an approach strengthens your sense of identity and your self-worth. Real forgiveness also demonstrates that you have choices, that you can make decisions, and that you will act decisively.

And perhaps this needn't be said, but always employ forgiveness—especially to the point of reconciliation—with wisdom. Forgiveness is not placing yourself in a position to be harmed again and again and again. Neither is it setting yourself up to be repeatedly disappointed. Don't enable the other person to continue in destructive behaviors at your expense.

You should also understand that the possibility for repeating an offense increases when offenders show no remorse and fail to seek any understanding or insight into their abusive behavior. Overlooking this fact can place you, the forgiver, at greater risk for continued abuse. In these cases, you must establish firm boundaries and place an appropriate distance between yourself and the offender.

So, again, beware of offering forgiveness when doing so weakens your sense of self and makes you feel like less of a person. Forgiveness should always empower you and make you feel better about yourself. This distinction is a good self-test for seeing whether your forgiveness is genuine or an unhealthy mutation.

6. Beware of social pressure to forgive.

As I said earlier, no one can decide when it's time for you to forgive; that is your decision and yours alone. But rest assured that others *will* suggest a timetable that stipulates the proper moment to forgive. Family members, work associates, church members, and best friends can and will put pressure on you to forgive so they don't have to experience any tension or conflict over the unforgiven event. You may not be ready to forgive, but they will try to force you—for their own good, not for yours. Family peace is more important to them than your peace.

Of course, I'm not recommending a flat and permanent refusal to forgive; I'm just reminding you that the timing of the choice to forgive is yours alone. Besides, forcing someone to forgive does not yield real forgiveness, but rather mandatory compliance— and, more than likely, a resentful compliance that creates a grievance story of its own. Anytime one individual tries to force forgiveness upon another, the results will be caustic and destructive, as seeds of bitterness are sown that will bear fruit for years to come. Don't do it.

7. Don't offer forgiveness on behalf of someone else.

It's tempting to want to help the offender and say something like, "I know Mary forgives you because she wants this marriage to work." But you cannot forgive on Mary's behalf; only she can do that work.

The problem becomes even more complex when a group of people has wronged another group of people. Can one African American, for instance, offer forgiveness on behalf of a whole generation of African Americans who were enslaved? Can one Bosnian mother offer forgiveness on behalf of all mothers whose children were murdered in an ethnic cleansing? The answer is a resounding no. No one can offer forgiveness on behalf of someone else. Only the person who was harmed can forgive.

For, at its heart, forgiveness takes place between two individuals. You can forgive only on behalf of yourself.

8. Don't offer forgiveness that leaves you feeling guiltier.

Sometimes when forgiveness is offered, a subtle shift of blame leaves the forgiver feeling worse. The forgiver's distorted thinking can go like this: *if the offenders are forgiven, then maybe what they did was not all that bad.* In fact, some false forms of forgiveness can shift responsibility from the one who did wrong to the one who was wronged.

Occasionally offenders interpret your attempts at reconciliation as a sign of weakness. They may then manipulate your efforts to show how wrong you were, in effect shifting blame. "What do you mean, you forgive me?" they might demand. "Your hands aren't completely clean in this! I should be the one forgiving you. If you hadn't said or done what you did, none of this would ever have happened." And so the offenders turn the tables; they take advantage of your vulnerability in approaching them to strengthen their position.

If you feel more at fault after offering forgiveness, then you have not experienced genuine forgiveness. And if you ever find yourself in this predicament, stay focused on how the other person's actions impacted you. They cannot change that reality no matter how they attempt to twist their account.

CHOOSE THE GENUINE ARTICLE

The flawed expressions of forgiveness we just looked at promise short-term fixes, but each one of them will leave you with long-term problems. In contrast, genuine forgiveness may take time, but its long-lasting and far-reaching results are worth it.

Remember that you don't have to do all the steps of forgiveness exactly right. After all, you can't script the other person's response. You simply need to do the best you can. Forgiveness does not remove pain; rather, it moves into and through the pain.

So stick with the genuine article. Avoid the counterfeits. And enjoy the profound benefits that true forgiveness offers you.

ASSIGNMENT

1. Think of a time when your attempt to forgive did not result in an apology, restitution, reconciliation, and continuing with the relationship.

2. Apply to that situation what you now know about forgiveness (specifically the eight cautions discussed in this chapter). What would you do differently today if you suddenly found yourself in that situation?

TWELVE

LIVING THE
FORGIVING LIFE

Do unto others what you would have them do unto you.
—The Golden Rule

The cover of the Winter 1999 issue of *Spirituality and Health* featured a picture of three United States servicemen, all former prisoners of war, standing in front of the Vietnam Veterans Memorial in Washington, DC. One soldier asked another, "Have you forgiven your captors yet?" The second one replied, "No, never!" And the third man turned and said, "Then it seems like they still have you in prison, don't they?"

Are you still trapped in the prison of your own painful past? The words regarding forgiveness that you have read in this book are nothing more than ideas and concepts—until you find yourself confronted by some painful reality that is destroying your life. Then these words function as essential principles of life that can spell the difference between joy and bitterness, success and failure, freedom and imprisonment. And what I'm talking about is far worse than a prison with four walls. I'm talking about the prison of your mind where your thoughts reduce your options and make you feel trapped by your circumstances.

Countless people have reached this crossroad and found forgiveness to be the only viable solution. Dr. Martin Luther King Jr., for example, chose the pathway of forgiveness at a crucial time in his life when he could have easily felt trapped by circumstances. In the face of deep-seated prejudice and as the frequent target of violent acts, Dr. King taught—and, more importantly, lived—forgiveness. He never excused the actions of the offenders, but rather revealed their weaknesses and true character. "Forgiveness is not an occasional act," he insisted; "it is a permanent attitude." Dr. King continued: "We must develop and maintain the capacity to forgive. He who is devoid of the power to forgive is devoid of the power to love."

Dr. King read much of the work of another great world leader who taught and lived forgiveness as a way of dealing with human evil. When confronted by superior British forces that sought to suppress the people of India, Mahatma Gandhi said, "The weak can never forgive. Forgiveness is the attribute of the strong." Later he went on to say: "If we practice an eye for an eye and a tooth for a tooth, soon the whole world will be blind and toothless."

FROM TACTICAL TO LIFE TRANSFORMING

Up to this point in the book, we've been looking at forgiveness as a way to effectively deal with a specific, hurtful event. And that's important. But that is only one aspect of forgiveness. I want to wrap things up by talking about something much broader and more important.

Forgiveness is a tool that, when used regularly, enables you to handle life rather than be overwhelmed by it. So the ultimate goal of living the forgiving life is to move from forgiveness as a tactic for coping with a specific conflict to forgiveness as a strategy for living. As you work to achieve this goal, you may find it helpful—as I have—to keep in mind the following two principles:

1. The more important forgiveness is to you, the more likely you are to forgive.

2. The more often you practice forgiveness, the more forgiving you become.

The goal of living the forgiving life is for forgiveness to become so much a part of who you are that when things do go wrong, you're already in a forgiving mode, so the problem doesn't have a chance of growing into a story of resentment. After all, it's always easier to prevent a problem than to fix it later.

FORGIVENESS: STATE OR TRAIT

Forgiveness can therefore be seen as either a *state* or a *trait*. The latter tends to grow out of the former.

- *State* forgiveness is something you do in response to an unwanted situation.

- *Trait* forgiveness is a part of who you are; it's a characteristic, an integral component of your personal makeup.

The moment of actually forgiving a specific wrong is state forgiveness. It involves the intentional letting go of negative thoughts and seeking a more compassionate view of the offender.

Trait forgiveness, however, is a personality characteristic that helps prevent the buildup of resentment and anger before those emotions have a chance to take a hold of your daily thoughts and feelings. Such an attitude comes from the awareness that other people struggle just as you do. It does not expect perfection. It understands that life is not fair and seeks to make the best of it.

The final phase of forgiveness therefore involves moving from state forgiveness to trait forgiveness. The transition happens once you stop seeing forgiveness as a tool for coping with a particular conflict or crisis and instead make it a regular life practice.

In other words, forgiveness is more than the development of a skill for dealing with specific problems. It is a journey toward a more meaningful life. Forgiveness requires regular practice, and it is strengthened by the positive reinforcement of others who are on the same journey.

THE BENEFITS OF TRAIT FORGIVENESS

According to a recent Gallup poll, people who are willing and able to forgive tend to be more satisfied with life. This finding reminds me of a statement I once saw on a poster: "Forgiveness is giving up all hope for a better past." Forgiveness does not change your past. Instead, it changes your feelings about the past so that you can walk boldly into the future.

Furthermore, an orientation toward forgiveness reduces the number of times you'll have to forgive in the first place. When you fully realize that you always have the option to forgive, you also realize that you have the choice *not* to take offense in the first place. And when you don't take offense at what someone else does or says, you will have fewer incidents in your life that are difficult to forgive.

With such an orientation toward forgiveness, you *automatically* reframe the situation when something goes wrong. You *automatically* look at how the incident is making you feel. You *automatically* ask yourself how you are going to let this affect your future. You *automatically* prevent the buildup of a grievance story and spare yourself the hard work of having to reframe it later.

Making forgiveness a habitual way of thinking means that you've shifted your worldview. You know that life *isn't* fair, so when bad things do occur, they do not turn your world upside down as they have in the past. In fact, you expect bad things to happen; you even anticipate them. And before they ever take place, you're prepared to deal with them.

Such an attitude completely changes your experience of life. It doesn't take away the hurt, the disruption, or the undesirability of the offense, but it gives you the ability to deal with the offense rather than be overwhelmed by it. With this orientation toward forgiveness, you refuse to expend a whole lot of energy thinking about how others have wronged you. Instead you use your energy to focus on what you need to do to achieve your most important life goals.

After all, the primary question you must answer is not "Why is my life the way it is?" but rather "What do I want my life to be like?" Your winning should be more important to you than the other person's losing—and trait forgiveness helps you to live that way.

While none of us can know for sure where life will take us, we do know there will be potholes and detours along the way. To think that your life will be perfect and nothing will ever go wrong is a serious self-deception. So, since you know you will need to forgive someone in the future, why not practice forgiveness every chance you get? Become an expert at living the forgiving life. Each time you forgive, it becomes easier to forgive the next time. Forgiveness is like a muscle: the more it is exercised, the more it can do. And the more you practice forgiving the little hurts in life, the better you will be able to handle the big hurts.

Also, since wounds take time to heal, realize that you may need to walk through the forgiveness process many times in order to come to terms with certain hurtful events. But each time you successfully forgive that nasty event from your past, you'll find it easier to release the hurt and reduce the impact of that event on your life. Each time you repeat the forgiveness cycle, the power of your grievance story is weakened.

WHERE ARE YOU HEADED?

I hope by this point you've already put into practice some of the skills and strategies you've read about and that you're walking the healing path of forgiveness. The following "Construct of Forgiveness" may help you assess where you are on this journey. The discussion explains the four possibilities.

Your attempts to forgive have likely taken you into one of four zones. Which zone you're in depends on the amount of effort you and the person who offended you have invested—or failed to invest—in the process. Let's take a brief look at each of these zones of forgiveness.

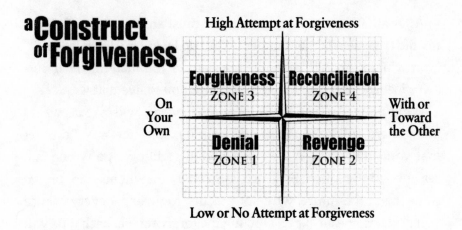

Zone 1: Denial

If you don't feel like forgiving and if the other person doesn't care about receiving your forgiveness, then neither one of you is facing reality. You may be hoping that by ignoring the situation it will somehow magically disappear. But when you have been deeply hurt, the saying "Time heals all wounds" does not apply. On the other hand, you may not forgive because you believe you cannot or should not forgive until the offender asks for forgiveness. Of course, as you have come to realize, this request for forgiveness may never come. So, at the end of the day, you are left holding the red-hot rock. Denial simply does not work. It can't work, for rather than bringing healing, it is nothing more than an attempt to escape the pain, a pain that will not go away by itself.

Living in this zone will ultimately lead to depression and withdrawal from life.

Zone 2: Revenge

If you find yourself in this zone, you aren't seeing any effort by the other to reform or even apologize for the hurtful words or actions that were directed at you. You have given up all hope of improving the relationship. The other person sees any attempt on your part to forgive as a weakness and feels free to continue their undesired behaviors. When you finally realize that the other person is going to do nothing to right the wrong done to you, then the desire for some sort of retaliation or revenge will start to take over your thinking. This desire will arise out of your inner conviction that life must be fair, so when it isn't, you feel the need to do something to make it right.

Living in this zone will lead only to your own destruction. You are still holding the red-hot rock, and you are doing so with a purpose, namely, that one day you can throw it back at the one who hurt you. As you wait, you alone suffer.

Living in this zone will leave you an angry, bitter person.

Zone 3: Forgiveness

As we've seen, forgiveness provides enormous benefits to the one who chooses to forgive. Your genuine forgiveness of those who have hurt you is important to your health and well-being. Why should you destroy your own life by dwelling on vengeful thoughts, regardless of how much the offender might deserve to face consequences of some kind?

Living in this zone will allow you to let go of the past and get on with life. This is dropping the rock!

Zone 4: Reconciliation

For most of us, forgiveness does not feel complete until the relationship is restored. This is most likely to happen when the offender acknowledges the wrong, offers apologies, asks for forgiveness, demonstrates remorse, and takes corrective action to right the wrong as much as possible.

If you are the offended party, you can often encourage this response by changing your angry attitude. Your change increases the chances that people around you will also change. Your expressions of forgiveness can stimulate repentance in the other, and then you both win. And even when reconciliation isn't possible because the offender refuses to admit the wrong, apologize to you, and ask your forgiveness, you can still benefit by extending forgiveness to him or her.

When the offender and the offended both choose forgiveness,

living in this zone will lead to a restored relationship that often can be stronger than it was before. But remember, it takes two to play this game.

A Spiritual Journey

In this book I have intentionally taken you down a path of personal forgiveness as if there were no other realities than your own healing and well-being.

But there are other realities. While personal forgiveness is the first step, it is not the last. I chose to focus on personal forgiveness in this book for three reasons. First, it is the dimension of forgiveness over which you have the most control. It is not dependent upon anyone else, so this kind of forgiveness has the best chance of actually happening. Second, personal forgiveness provides you with the most immediate benefits that will affirm your efforts. Finally, I chose to focus on personal forgiveness because its benefits are the easiest to measure. Yet, in many ways, personal forgiveness is only the starting place for the other dimensions of forgiveness. Aware that we all start at different places and with different belief systems, I have attempted to make forgiveness as relevant to every individual as I could.

But I must emphasize that forgiveness is ultimately a spiritual experience. I cannot discuss meaning and purpose in life without moving into the spiritual realm. I believe we are all spiritual creatures who seek meaning and purpose in life. We are not content to merely eat, sleep, and mate like the rest of the animal kingdom. No, we are creatures of meaning. We think beyond the visible constructs. We long to be a part of something greater than ourselves. And this is what makes us spiritual.

Gallup polls inform us that most Americans first experienced forgiveness when they received God's forgiveness of their sins. A few years ago you could hardly watch a sporting event without seeing someone in the crowd holding up a poster that read simply

"John 3:16." That well-known text from the Bible reminded millions and millions of individuals that while we were yet sinners, God forgave us—in fact, His Son died for us—so that we could be free from the chains of our past, so that we could be forgiven. The perspective offered by that single verse from Scripture frames reality in the largest context possible: today's daily choices do indeed have eternal consequences.

I recognize that not all my readers are necessarily religious, and that is fine. But all my readers—including you—are spiritual, and spiritual individuals recognize that they are no longer chained to their past. Spiritual people also understand that they have the opportunity and the ability to live for tomorrow. They see eternal significance in the temporal and thus have the broadest frame of reference in which to place their life. Spiritual individuals live each day in the context of a greater purpose in life.

Spiritual individuals also understand that living with an eye toward possibilities is much more rewarding than living preoccupied with one's problems. They can't understand why anyone would choose to remain trapped in the troubles of their yesterdays when a whole lifetime of dazzling tomorrows beckons. So, through forgiveness, these spiritual individuals let go and move on.

You can too.

A JOURNEY WITH DEEP REWARDS

As eighteenth-century Dutch physician Paul Boese once said: "Forgiveness does not change the past, but it does enlarge the future." It is my hope that, as a result of reading this book, your life will become more rewarding, your health improved, and your future brighter. Forgiveness is a journey—and the deeper the wounds, the longer the journey. But it is a journey that offers significant rewards along the way. As you travel the pathway of forgiveness, think about the following words that speak deeply of the spiritual life:

The only effective response to the past is forgiveness,
the only effective response to the present is love,
and the only effective response to the future is hope.
Continue your journey of forgiveness today—and each and every day into the future. You *can* live the forgiving life. You can forgive to live!

ASSIGNMENT

1. When you teach something, you benefit from the experience as much or even more than the people you teach. Teaching others reinforces what you have learned. So your assignment is to teach others about forgiveness.

2. Take "The Forgiveness Journey" test again (reprinted below) and see how you score this time. Celebrate your progress on your journey by living the forgiving life.

THE FORGIVENESS JOURNEY

Answer the following questions as honestly as you can. It will help you to know where you are on your forgiveness journey.

	YES	NO
1. Do you have a story about someone who has wronged you, someone whom you have yet to forgive?	—	—
2. Are you aware of the price you are paying by not forgiving?	—	—
3. Have you made the choice to forgive?	—	—
4. Are you able to sufficiently change your story of hurt and suffering so it is less painful?	—	—
5. Has your new story of the old event given you a better perspective on life?	—	—

6. When a situation brings you back to feeling helpless, are you able to change that feeling?   __ __

7. Are you making progress toward achieving the goals you have set for yourself?   __ __

8. Are you more understanding of the other person's circumstances even though you disagree with what he or she did?   __ __

9. Have you reconciled with the person involved?   __ __

10. Has forgiveness brought you peace with God or greater clarity about your higher purpose in life?   __ __

Now go back to the end of chapter 1 to see how you answered these same questions earlier. Where are your answers the same and where are they different? Focus your attention and efforts on those aspects of forgiveness you haven't yet mastered, but also celebrate the growth you've experienced. Your life will never be the same. After all, with each successful step along the journey comes the possibility of taking the next step toward fully living the forgiving life.

APPENDIX

HYPERTENSION REDUCTION THROUGH FORGIVENESS TRAINING

For those who are interested, I am including in this appendix a report on the forgiveness study I conducted at Florida Hospital. The study—formally approved by an internal review board made up of physicians, nurses, lawyers, and community leaders—is presented here as it was published in the *Journal of Pastoral Care and Counseling* (Spring-Summer 2006, Vol. 60, Nos. 1–2). The paper was written for an academic audience, and I have not altered it for this book. I realize that not every reader will want to wade through the data, jargon, and design issues of the study, so let me offer you the basic conclusions now.

- Forgiveness does not cure all heart disease. The study showed that forgiveness can be clinically effective in reducing anger; and for people whose elevated anger level is contributing to their hypertension, practicing forgiveness proved to be an effective intervention for reducing blood pressure.

- The study should not encourage anyone with high blood pressure to throw away medications in favor of practicing forgiveness. High blood pressure can result from a large number of

175

factors, of which suppressed anger and hostility is simply one important variable.

- You've probably heard that a number of practices (weight management, regular aerobic exercise, reducing the salt in your diet, etc.) can help you lower your blood pressure. You should consider all of these options as well as forgiveness. Of course, before you embark on any health program, you should always consult your physician.

The bottom line of the forgiveness study is this: people's health and lives were measurably improved when they practiced forgiveness. Thus the title of this book: *Forgive to Live.* Now to the study.

ABSTRACT

The objective of this study was to determine if patients with diagnosed stage-1 hypertension could benefit by a forgiveness training program to achieve measurable reductions in anger expression and blood pressure. Twenty-five participants were randomly divided into wait-listed control and intervention groups. The control group monitored blood pressure while the intervention group participated in an eight-week forgiveness training program. At the end of eight weeks, the wait-listed group became an intervention group. Those who received forgiveness training achieved significant reductions in anger expression when compared to the control group. While reductions in blood pressure were not achieved by all the participants, those participants who entered the program with elevated anger expression scores did achieve significant reductions in blood pressure. It is suggested that forgiveness training may be an effective clinical intervention for some hypertensive patients with elevated levels of anger.

INTRODUCTION

It is estimated that about 30 percent of the United States population has hypertension, with the risk increasing as one ages.[1] In 1991, more than 40 percent of all deaths in the US were associated with cardiac and vascular disease, for which hypertension is a major risk factor.[2] The standard cardiovascular disease risk factors (Ht, smoking, hyper-lipidemia) predict fewer than half the new cases of coronary heart disease.[3] This is because hypertension is a multifactoral problem needing interventions that address multiple root causes.[4] The complex etiology of the disease includes genetic, environmental, lifestyle, and psychological factors which can interact in a variety of ways.[5]

Stress, the perception of stress, and the lack of ability to cope with stress result in increased sympathetic activity which in turn increases vascular resistance and elevates blood pressure.[6] Stress management programs have had some degree of success in lowering blood pressure.[7] However, large deviations in the meta-analysis of stress-management techniques indicate that treatments were effective in some cases but ineffective in others.[8] It therefore becomes necessary to identify and characterize sub-populations of those facing various types of life stressors to understand these variations.

There is a body of literature suggesting that the ways people respond to interpersonal offenses can affect health.[9] Initially the focus was on personality type, particularly the relationship between Type-A personality and heart disease.[10] Later findings suggest it was not the Type-A behavior that was the causal factor; rather it was underlying anger and resentment.[11] This association between anger and coronary heart disease was identified in the Framingham Heart Study.[12] Recent research continues to link anger, blame, hostility, and resentment with negative health outcomes.[13]

Coronary heart disease is especially linked with unforgiving responses.[14] It is becoming evident that one's cognitive processes and internal dialogue contribute to elevated blood pressure. For example, people can "work themselves up" by the thoughts they rehearse in their minds, which in turn, can lead to higher blood pressure.[15]

One way of changing the beliefs that underlie the negative self-talk is to forgive. In fact, learning and applying forgiveness has been shown to reduce anger.[16] Unforgiving responses (rehearsing the hurt or retaining the grudge) activate negative intense emotions which in turn cause sympathetic nervous system reactivity,[17] whereas forgiving responses (empathizing with the offender or granting forgiveness) can reverse these physiological reactions.[18] In one study, participants who simply visualized an upsetting memory experienced significantly greater sympathetic nervous system arousal as indicated by higher skin conductance, increased heart rate, and elevated blood pressure. When they then visualized the same upsetting memory while imagining what it would be like to forgive that incident, they reversed all the measured physiological symptoms.[19] Another recent study using functional magnetic resonance imaging seems to suggest that by thinking about forgiveness, neuro-activity is changed in a region of the brain that responds only to forgiveness.[20]

Based upon existing evidence, it would appear logical that teaching the process of forgiveness to individuals with high blood pressure, who also tend to harbor unforgiving responses, would result in lowered blood pressure. This study aims to investigate the effect forgiveness training may have on lowering levels of anger expression, and in turn, lowering blood pressure for patients diagnosed with stage-1 hypertension.

One of the challenges in using forgiveness as an independent variable is that there is no standard definition of forgiveness.[21] The forgiveness principles used in this study draw from religious traditions as well as from psychological constructs describing the behavioral and cognitive tasks involved in the process of forgiveness.[22] The definition of forgiveness developed for use in this study is as follows: the process of reframing one's anger from the past, with the goal of recovering one's peace in the present and revitalizing one's purpose for the future. In this way one learns how to deal with the past offenses, which can lead to current emotional disturbances, and ultimately to perceived limitations on the future.

METHODS

An eight-week forgiveness training program was developed by the authors specifically for this study using cognitive, emotional, behavioral, and spiritual principles. Through group discussion and support, forgiveness principles would be identified by each participant, based on their needs, and then applied to specific hurts. The lessons learned would then be rehearsed and reinforced through homework assignments.

In week one the participants learned basic mind and body connections so they could begin to understand how certain thoughts and emotions affect physiology, particularly the heart. In week two they learned how to change their thoughts through visualization to achieve a different emotional response. In week three the focus was on how anger begins and is maintained through the retelling of grievance stories. In the fourth week participants learned how to reframe their grievance story so that it could be modified with the goal of altering the emotional response. In the fifth week participants began to understand how retaining the hurt was more damaging to their health than they may have realized. In week six, all the positive benefits of forgiveness were identified as opposed to not forgiving. Discussion also focused on the possibility of reconciliation with the offender, but affirmed that would require the participation of two willing individuals, which may or may not be possible. Week seven was a review week to both reinforce what was learned as well as to make up any missed sessions due to absence. In the final week the discussion focused on maintaining forgiveness as a way of life. The core principle was to move from victim to victor because of the release experienced by forgiveness.

SUBJECTS

This study was approved by Florida Hospital's internal review board. Twenty-five participants were screened to meet certain inclusion criteria: twenty-one-plus-year-old male or non-pregnant female with an established diagnosis of stage-1 hypertension—diastolic reading of 90 to 99 mmHG and/or a systolic reading of 140 to 159 mmHG22. Participants were excluded if they were: currently under treatment for cancer, on psychotropic medications, had documented chronic renal insufficiency and/or creatinine level greater than 1.9, on blood pressure medications, had diabetes mellitus, heart disease (left ventricular hypertrophy, angina/prior myocardial infarction, prior coronary revascularization, and/or heart failure), or a prior history of stroke or transient ischemic attack, nephropathy, peripheral arterial disease, and/or retinopathy.

All participants attended an orientation session to discuss protocol and sign an informed consent. Participants were randomly assigned to either a control group (N=13) or an intervention group (N=12). At the start of the study each participant was administered the State-Trait Anger Expression Inventory test-2 (STAXI-2) which measures the expression and control of anger.[23] For the purposes of this study we focused on the anger-expression score. This measure was chosen because it was believed that anger expression could be more easily observed and thus understood by the participants. This test was administered at the beginning of the study and again at the end of the study.

PROCEDURES

Each participant was given a digital blood-pressure monitor to take home (courtesy of Omron Healthcare, Inc. and instructed by a nurse how to take blood-pressure readings according to instructions supplied. Throughout the sixteen-week study each participant took two blood-pressure readings five minutes apart on Monday, Wednesday, and Friday at a consistent time they chose and then mailed their readings each week. The participants took their blood pressure at home, instead of in class, as taking blood-pressure readings in a medical setting may actually increase blood pressure.[24] Another benefit of regular home monitoring was to obtain a sufficient number of readings to ensure trend data rather than isolated readings, which can be subject to wide variation. The mean arterial pressure (MAP), was then calculated by using the formula [(systolic * 2) + diastolic] / 3.

The intervention group participated in an eight-week forgiveness training workshop led by a chaplain while the wait-listed control group simply monitored their blood pressure from home. At the completion of the forgiveness training program, the intervention group continued to monitor their blood pressure for an additional two months. After eight-weeks of monitoring blood pressure the wait-listed control group then became an intervention group.

The forgiveness training lasted for one and a half hours and each group met one night a week over eight consecutive weeks. The format each week consisted of the following components: review of the previous week's assignment with opportunity for questions and clarification, introduction of new material by lecture and workbook activity, group interaction and reaction to new material, and new assignments for rehearsal at home. Each participant would share their progress and would have an opportunity to express and clarify their understanding and application of forgiveness.

RESULTS

Analysis of the data showed a significant reduction in the mean score on the anger expression index score—utilizing the STAXI-2 scales—after participation in forgiveness training. The t-test for paired samples was employed to analyze the data. The group mean change in anger expression scores, as a result of the forgiveness training, dropped from 13.00 (sd = 11.77) to 1.83 (sd = 5.81). The obtained t-score was -3.19 (p = .004), indicating that the group mean anger expression scores were significantly reduced after participation in the forgiveness training program. As a group, this represents a drop from moderately high anger expression scores to a little

Table #1

t-Scores

Var	N	X_1	Sd	X_2	Sd	t
Anger Expression	25	13.00	11.77	1.83	5.81	-3.19
Mean Arterial Pressure	25	133.26	1.37	131.05	1.66	-0.42

N = number of participants in the program
X_1 = the average score of all participants at the beginning of the program
X_2 = the average score of all participants at the end of the program
Sd = standard deviation
t = a score derived from paired sampling

lower than the normal range of anger expression scores as indicated by STAXI-2 normative scales.

Forgiveness training did not lead to significant reductions in MAP for the intervention group as a whole. The *t*-test for paired samples was employed to analyze the data. The group mean MAP before and after the training program were 133.26 (sd = 1.37) and 131.05 (sd = 1.66) respectively. The obtained *t*-score was -0.42 (p = .68). While the decrease in blood pressure was not clinically significant for the group as a whole, it is interesting to observe that there was a slight decrease in the blood-pressure readings within the intervention group as a result of the forgiveness training.

What is of significance to note, is that upon further analysis of the data, a positive correlation between reduction in anger expression and reduction in blood pressure was identified. The obtained *r*-value, a measure of correlation, was .47 (p = .02). This analysis demonstrated a statistically significant relationship between reductions in anger expression and reductions in MAP after participation in forgiveness training among subjects who scored high on the anger expression scale. More specifically, the obtained *r*-value indicated that the greater the reduction in anger expression, the greater the reduction in blood pressure. This would indicate that those with elevated anger received the most benefit in blood-pressure

Table #2

The Correlation of Anger Expression Reduction with Blood-Pressure Reduction

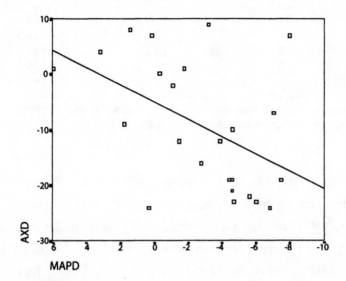

AXD is the difference between the anger expression score (AX) from week eight subtracted from the (AX) score of week one. A negative number represents a reduction in anger expression.

MAPD is the difference between the Mean Arterial Pressure (MAP) reading taken at week eight subtracted from the (MAP) reading taken at week one. A negative number represents a reduction in blood pressure.

Each square plots each participant in the study. The direction of the line indicates a correlation whereby the greater the reduction in anger expression, the more likely there will be a reduction in blood pressure.

reduction as a result of the forgiveness training. In fact, those with the largest declines in their anger expression scores did achieve the highest drops in blood pressure as seen in the table that rank ordered participants by reductions in anger expression scores.

DISCUSSION

No published study was found that demonstrates sustained drops in blood pressure for stage-1 hypertensive patients through the use

Table #3

Actual Blood-Pressure Readings of Forgiveness Training Participants

Participant #	AXD Reduction	Beginning BP	Ending BP
108	34	144/97	130/81
127	28	154/98	124/76
126	26	151/99	132/86
121	26	157/107	123/84
133	19	153/87	124/80

The above chart shows the top five participants in terms of rank ordering from the highest reduction in anger expression score to lowest.

of forgiveness training as a clinical intervention. While lowering blood pressure through participation in forgiveness training will not benefit all with high blood pressure, those with elevated levels of anger may benefit. When those with both high blood pressure and elevated anger were identified and taught how to forgive, reductions in blood pressure were achieved. Given the complex, multifactoral causes of hypertension, it would be helpful to diagnose those hypertensive patients with elevated anger in order to identify those who could most likely benefit by forgiveness training.

It would be inappropriate to conclude from this study that forgiveness training can reverse high blood pressure for all people, or even all those with elevated anger. The sample size was too small to come to any definitive conclusions. Yet the beneficial findings of this study warrant further investigation with a larger sample size.

There is always the possibility that this study did not measure what we thought it did. For example, we could be measuring the positive effects of group support instead of forgiveness as the beneficial variable. However, blood-pressure readings taken two months after the forgiveness training indicated the blood pressures continued to drop slightly after the group support was discontinued. If group support were the operative variable, one would expect a reversion back toward the initial mean.

While forgiveness was taught, and assignments were given to

reinforce the learning, there was no measurement used in this study to determine if forgiveness had actually taken place. It was assumed, but not proven, that if anger scores declined, the operative agent was forgiveness. Given the lack of consensus on a definition of forgiveness, there is consequently no widely accepted standardized instrument for measuring forgiveness.[25] An effective tool to measure forgiveness, as taught in this program, will be necessary in a future study, in order to measure how successfully forgiveness was learned and applied. However, in participant taped interviews conducted at the end of each forgiveness training program, many of the participants stated that the instruction they had received on forgiveness was helpful to them in forgiving others as well as in forgiving themselves.

It would have also been helpful to measure the frequency with which forgiveness was practiced. We had no way of knowing how much rehearsal was taking place utilizing the forgiveness principles. Thus we were not able to measure any differences in success based on differences in compliance with the forgiveness assignments.

This study seeks to lay a foundation for the eventual standardization of forgiveness training so that some day chaplains and other clinicians can confidently recommend hypertensive patients, screened for elevated anger, to appropriate forgiveness training programs for the self-management of high blood pressure.

ENDNOTES TO THE APPENDIX

1. M. J. Horan, "Introduction: Hypertension Research Perspective in the United States," *Health Psychology*, 1988, Vol. 7, pp. 9–14.

2. E. J. Branwald, E. Braunwald, and N. K. Holenberg, *Atlas of Heart Disease: Hypertension Mechanisms and Therapy* (Philadelphia, PA: Current Medicine, 1995).

3. N. Schneiderman, M. A. Chesney, and D. S. Krantz, "Biobehavioral Aspects of Cardiovascular Disease; Progress and Prospects," *Health Psychology*, 1989, Vol. 8, pp. 649–76.

4. P. Hamet, Z. Pausova, V. Adairichev, K. Adairichev, and J. Tremblay, "Hypertension: Genes and Environment," *Journal of Hypertension*, 1998, Vol. 6, pp. 397–418.

5. I. H. Pages, "Some Regulatory Mechanisms of Renovascular and Essential Hypertension," in J. Genest, E. Koiw, O. Kuchel, (Eds.). *Hypertension: Physiopathology and Treatment* (New York: McGraw-Hill, 1997), pp. 576–87.

6. S. Jern, V. Wall, and A. Bergbrandt, "Long-Term Stability of Blood Pressure and Pressure Activity to Mental Stress in Borderline Hypertension," *American Journal of Hypertension*, 1995, Vol. 8, pp. 20–28.

7. M. P. Garciavera, F. J. Labrador, and J. Sanz, "Stress Management Training for Essential Hypertension: A Controlled Study," *Applied Psychophysiology and Biofeedback*, 1997, Vol. 22, pp. 261–83.

8. M. M. Ward, G. E. Swan, and M. A. Chesney, "Arousal-Reduction Treatments for Mild Hypertension: A Meta-Analysis of Recent Studies," in J. Bassett and D. R. Bassett (Eds.). *Handbook of Hypertension: Behavioral Focus in Hypertension* (Amsterdam: Elsevier, 1987), pp. 285–302.

9. C. E. Thoresen, F. Luskin, and A. H. S. Harris, "Science and Forgiveness Interventions: Reflections and Recommendations," in E. L. Worthington, Jr., (Ed.). *Dimensions of Forgiveness* (Philadelphia: Templeton Foundation Press, 1998), pp. 163–69.

10. M. Freidman, C. E. Thoresen, J. J. Gill, L. H. Powell, D. Ulmer, L. Thompson, et al., "Alteration of Type A Behavior and Reduction in Cardiac Recurrences in Postmyocardial Infarction Patients," *American Heart Journal*, 1984, Vol. 108, pp. 237–48.

11. L. H. Powell and C. E. Thoresen, "Behavioral and Physiologic Determinants of Long-Term Prognosis After Myocardial Infarction," *Journal of Chronic Disease*, 1985, Vol. 38, p. 253.

12. S. G. Hayes, M. Feinleib, and W. B. Kannel, "The Relationship of Psychosocial Factors to Coronary Heart Disease in the Framingham Study, III: 8-Year Incidence of Coronary Heart Disease," *American Journal of Epidemiology*, 1980, Vol. 111, pp. 37–58.

13. J. E. Williams, C. C. Paton, C. Siegler, M. L. Eigenbrodt, F. J. Nieto, and H. A. Tyroler, "Anger Proneness Predicts Coronary Heart Disease Risk: Prospective Analysis from the Atherosclerosis Risk in Communities (ARIC) Study," *Circulation*, 2000, Vol. 101, pp. 2034–39.

14. T. Q. Miller, T. W. Smith, C. W. Turner, M. L. Guijarro, A. J. Haller, "Meta-Analytic Review of Research on Hostility and Physical Health," *Psychological Bulletin*, 1996, Vol. 119, pp. 322–48.

15. A. T Beck, *Depression: Clinical Experimental and Theoretical Aspects* (New York: Harper and Row, 1967).

16. F. Luskin, *Forgive for Good: A Proven Prescription for Health and Happiness* (New York: Harper Collins Pub., Inc., 2002).

17. R. Williams and V. Williams, *Anger Kills: Seventeen Strategies for Controlling the Hostility That Can Harm Your Health* (New York: Harper Perennial, 1993).

18. C. E. Thoresen, A. H. S. Harris, and F. Luskin, "Forgiveness and Health: An Unanswered Question," in M. E. McCullough, K. I.

Pargament, and C. E. Thoresen, (Eds.), *Forgiveness: Theory, Research, and Practice* (New York: Guildford Press, 1999), pp. 254–80.

19. C. V. O. Witvliet, T. E. Ludwig, and K. L. Vander Laan, "Granting Forgiveness or Harboring Grudges: Implications for Emotion, Physiology, and Health," *Psychological Science*, 2001, Vol. 12, pp. 117–23.

20. T. F. Farrow, Y. Zheng, I. D. Wilkinson, S. A. Spence, J. F. Deakin, N. Tarrier, P. D. Griffiths, and P. W. Woodruff, "Investigating the Functional Anatomy of Empathy and Forgiveness," *Neuroreport*, 2001, Vol. 12, pp. 2433–38.

21. R. T. Denton and M. W. Martin, "Defining Forgiveness: An Empirical Exploration of Process and Role," *American Journal of Family Therapy*, 1998, Vol. 26, pp. 281–92.

22. National Institute of Health, *The Sixth Report of the Joint National Committee on Prevention, Detection, Evaluation, and Treatment of High Blood Pressure*, (Bethesda, MD: NIH publication No. 98-4080, 1997).

23. C. D. Spielberger, *STAXI-2 State-Trait Anger Expression Inventory-2: Professional Manual*, (Odessa, FL: Psychological Assessment Resources, Inc., 1999).

24. C. E. Lerman, D. S. Brody, T. Hui, C. Lazaro, D. G. Smith, and M. J. Blum, "The White-Coat Hypertension Response," *Journal General Internal Medicine*, 1989, Vol. 4, pp. 226–31.

25. M. E. McCullough, "Scales of Forgiveness," in P. Hill and R. Hood (Eds.), *Measures of Religiosity* (Birmingham, AL: Religious Education Press, 1999, pp. 457–64.

DISCUSSION GUIDE

ONE
LIFE SHOULD BE FAIR

1. In what way does the idea that life should be fair affect the way you live? Think of a recent event when life wasn't fair. How did you react?

2. Describe a time when something that seemed fair to someone else seemed very unfair to you. Do you see how fairness is in the eyes of the beholder?

3. What is your typical reaction when someone hurts you?

   • You try to win an apology.

   • You begin to resent the person who treated you unfairly.

   • You react with anger.

   • You fantasize revenge.

   • You withdraw.

   Why do you think you tend to act in this way? What usually happens when you react in this way?

4. Why isn't forgiveness "fair"? Why does the issue of fairness—of life *not* being fair—make it hard for us to forgive?

Two
My Life Is Your Fault

1. When something unfair happens to you, do you tend to blame or to forgive? Why?

2. Explain why the Blame Game leaves those who play it feeling completely helpless and stuck.

3. Do you believe that vengeance hurts you more than it does the other person? Why or why not?

4. Why does forgiveness enable you to move from victim to victor?

5. Why is it tempting to indulge in all-or-nothing thinking about someone who has hurt you?

6. Why is it important to distinguish between *intent* and *impact* when you're thinking about an unfair event in your life?

7. What can you do to begin to lower your expectations of others?

8. Who is responsible for your happiness? What practical implications does your answer have for your life?

Three
From Bitter to Better

1. Do you know an angry person? Why do you think of that person as being angry? Do you see yourself as an angry person? Why or why not?

2. When you get angry, what line of reasoning do you most often use to justify your anger?

3. Think of someone who has hurt you. What evil motives have you assigned to this person?

4. On the following scale of anger, where do you most often find your-self? Annoyed—Irritated—Upset—Hostile—Enraged—Resentful

5. Do you think you get angry more often than is necessary and/or do you stay angry longer than is helpful? Explain why you answered as you did.

6. What's good about your anger?

7. What's bad about your anger?

8. Which of the Seven Deadly Strategies for dealing with anger are you most likely to utilize? How effective has this strategy been for you?

9. Do you most naturally express your anger passively, aggres-sively, or assertively? Give details from your life that support your answer.

10. When someone hurts you, do you tend to express your hurt or your anger? Why? If you answered "anger," what can you do to train yourself to express your hurt rather than your anger?

FOUR
WHAT YOU TELL YOURSELF CAN KILL YOU

1. Describe a time when you interpreted an event or conversation one way only to discover later that what occurred or what was said could be understood differently.

2. What happened to your body when you squeezed your fist for five seconds? What happened differently when you squeezed your fist but laughed at the same time? What truth about the mind/body connection did this experiment teach or reinforce for you?

3. Respond to the following statement: "A person who is prone to anger is three times more likely to suffer from a heart attack than someone who is not prone to anger."

4. Explain the difference between acute anger and chronic anger. Which of the two normally presents the most medical challenges? Why?

5. Think of a person who has hurt you. What could—or will—you do to begin to change your perception of that individual?

6. If you could learn to forgive the person who hurt you, do you think you could lower your levels of anger? Why or why not?

7. Are you currently suffering from any physical symptoms that forgiveness might ease? If so, what are they? As you practice forgiveness, monitor your symptoms for any improvements. Note: Your symptoms may have other causes. If they persist, be sure to consult your physician.

FIVE
THE BIRTH OF A GRIEVANCE STORY

1. What stories have shaped your life?

2. Do you have a grievance story? If so, is it helping you or hurting you? Explain.

3. Think of a time when someone really hurt you.

   • What conclusions about yourself, about the other person, even about life did you draw from that event?

   • Did you take the offense more personally than you needed to? Explain your answer.

   • To whom and how often do you repeat this story? Why do you retell it?

4. Why do your grievance stories reopen old wounds? In what way do they handcuff you, the teller, to a person you don't even like?

5. Identify a grievance story from your own life.

   • What aspects of the story can you start to modify to better reflect reality?

   • Who controls the events in your story? Who's in charge of the outcome?

6. What evil motives does your grievance story assign to the person who hurt you?

7. When you evaluate the hurtful incident more carefully, what details emerge that once failed to show up in your grievance story?

8. What can you do to learn to act, rather than react, to the hurts inflicted on you by others?

SIX
FORGIVENESS IS A CHOICE

1. If you were in Simon Wiesenthal's place, what might have been your response to the dying Nazi soldier's request?

2. Why is it necessary for us to choose to forgive? Why can't forgiveness happen automatically?

3. Why does that pause between *stimulus* and *response* make us truly human? What interpretations, reflections, or decisions can we make during this pause?

4. Why does forgiveness line up with the core values of love, respect, and the desire for harmony and peace? Do you support these core values and desires? If so, what role—and how prominent a role—does forgiveness play in your life?

5. What destiny for yourself are you choosing by the decisions you're making today?

6. Are you ready to forgive the person who hurt you? Why or why not?

7. Have you placed forgiveness on your list of options? Why or why not?

SEVEN
IT'S NOT EASY TO FORGIVE

1. Has your inability to understand why someone hurt you made it harder for you to forgive that person? Explain.

2. Define *humility* and explain its connection to forgiveness.

3. Discuss why humility is a sign of strength, not weakness.

4. Identify a few of your own shortcomings and weaknesses. What mistakes have you made that hurt others? Who has forgiven you for these mistakes?

5. Think again about the event that prompted your grievance story. As you look at the event more carefully, what role might you have played in what happened?

6. Define *empathy*. Why is empathy able to pave the way for forgiveness?

7. Do what you can to walk a mile in the moccasins of the person who hurt you. Write down what you learn from doing this exercise.

8. What life experience(s) can help you better understand what the person who hurt you might have been thinking?

9. In what ways are you like the person who hurt you? In what ways are you different? Which list is longer—and why is that significant?

Eight
Forgiving by Reframing the Past

1. Explain why reality is what you remember it being.

2. Why can the process of forgiveness change your memory of a pain-filled past?

3. What does it mean to "reframe" your memories of the past?

4. Why is it significant that a grievance story uses the smallest possible frame?

5. Why does using a larger frame lead to a more accurate recall of the past?

6. What will you do to begin to think about the person who hurt you in a new, bigger-picture way?

7. It is impossible for us to:

   • Change the past

   • Change the other person

   • Make life fair

   Which of these impossibilities do you most often find yourself trying to achieve? What truths can you tell yourself to counter that tendency?

8. What do you need to do to let go of your hurtful past? Specifically, what needs to happen to your grievance story?

9. What are the six key steps to changing a painful memory?

10. If you ever have to revisit the process of reframing a painful memory, does that mean you have not truly forgiven? Explain.

NINE

FORGIVING AND FINDING PEACE IN THE PRESENT

1. Define *contentment*. Are you content? Put differently, does gratitude for what you have overshadow concern about what you lack and worry about what you want? Explain.

2. Why does experiencing peace in the present help you forgive?

3. What is your own internal default channel? Describe what you can do to change the channel when you don't want it playing in your mind.

4. Why does changing your thoughts also change your feelings? What thoughts are most likely to cause you painful feelings?

5. Try the diaphragmatic breathing exercise (pages 130–131). What happens to your thoughts and feelings when you breathe like this?

6. Try the progressive muscle relaxation technique (pages 132–133). What happens to your thoughts and feelings when you relax your muscles like this?

7. Do you consider being still a waste of time? Why or why not? Explain how stillness can help you do the hard work of forgiveness.

8. What have you noticed about how light affects your moods? What change can you make in the lighting around you to improve your outlook?

9. What colors tend to bring you feelings of peace? What colors tend to make you feel more anxious?

10. What aromas give you a sense of calm? Which ones make you feel agitated?

11. What will you do to use sound to help you achieve a more relaxed and peaceful environment at home? At work? In your car?

Ten
Forgiving and Finding Hope for the Future

1. Why does forgiveness help you move from what was to what can be?

2. Explain the connection between forgiveness and hope.

3. Do you tend toward "what if . . ." or "if only . . ." thinking? Why do you think that is?

4. Where are you going in life? Describe the future you desire.

5. What goals are helping you build that desired future? Be sure that they are:

   • Written

   • Specific

   • Sequenced

   • Measurable

   • Scheduled

6. What long-term goals have you set for yourself?

7. What intermediate goals must you establish in order to achieve your long-term goals?

8. Finally, what short-term steps do you need to take this month, this week, this very day in order to achieve your intermediate and ultimately your long-term goals?

9. What can you do to keep the urgent from crowding out the important? Be specific.

10. What practical steps can you take to keep a fear of failure from allowing you to move ahead toward your desired future?

Eleven
A Few Cautions

1. Do you ever offer forgiveness too quickly? Why? What can you do to avoid doing so?

2. Explain the unhealthy connection between forgiveness and one-upmanship.

3. In what way can people use forgiveness as a weapon?

4. Why can a false kind of forgiveness shut you off from your own feelings?

5. In what ways do some people use forgiveness to avoid confrontation? What is the problem with this strategy?

6. Explain how improper forgiveness can make someone vulnerable to revictimization.

7. What can you do to make sure that your forgiveness never costs you your sense of self-worth or your own well-being?

8. What kinds of social pressures to forgive might you experience? What can you do to effectively resist those pressures?

9. Have you ever tried to forgive someone on behalf of someone else? Why won't this work?

10. If offering forgiveness ever makes you feel guiltier, what has gone wrong?

Twelve
Living the Forgiving Life

1. What can you do to make forgiveness a permanent attitude, a foundational principle of your life? Be specific.

2. What is the difference between forgiveness as a tactic and forgiveness as a strategy?

3. On a scale of 1 to 10, with 10 being extremely important, how important is forgiveness to you? Why does it earn that ranking?

4. What can you do to move from offering forgiveness as something you do (a *state*) to forgiveness as something you are (a *trait*)?

5. Why do you think people who practice forgiveness report more satisfaction in life than those who do not?

6. Why does practicing forgiveness reduce the frequency of having to forgive in the first place?

7. Why does forgiving become easier with practice?

8. Take another look at "A Construct of Forgiveness." In which of the four zones do you spend most of your time? Do you like where you are, or would you rather be somewhere else? If you want to move, what will you have to do to make the change?

9. Explain why forgiveness is ultimately a spiritual journey.

10. Why does forgiveness give you the ability to live for tomorrow?

ABOUT THE AUTHOR

 Dr. Dick Tibbits has worked in the field of pastoral care and behavioral health for more than thirty years. He has used his training and experience in counseling to help tens of thousands of people achieve a better life. Dr. Tibbits has dedicated his life to whole-person health and designing life strategies that work in both the corporate world and private life.

Dr. Tibbits has a doctoral degree in psychology and is a licensed professional counselor. He is also an ordained minister with a master's degree in theology. He has served as an adjunct professor for doctoral students at both Fuller Theological Seminary and Andrews University Theological Seminary. Dr. Tibbits is a certified supervisor with the Association for Clinical Pastoral Education. In addition, Dr. Tibbits trained at the Harvard University Mind-Body-Spirit Institute and worked collaboratively with professors from Stanford University on his pioneering clinical research.

Dr. Tibbits has spoken on the healing power of forgiveness to professional and private audiences around the world, including Australia, New Zealand, Hong Kong, the Philippines, India, and Switzerland. He has presented his research at Harvard, Mayo, Stanford, and Loma Linda as well as to conferences as diverse as The International Conference on Stress and The National Woman's Health Conference. He has appeared on a number of radio and TV talk shows.

Dr. Tibbits currently serves as the Chief People Officer at Florida Hospital, the largest hospital in America.

To find out more about Dr. Tibbits's work, please visit him online at:

www.DickTibbits.com

For nearly one hundred years, the mission of Florida Hospital has been to help patients, guests, and friends achieve whole-person health and healing. With seven hospital campuses and sixteen walk-in medical centers, Florida Hospital cares for nearly one million patients every year.

Over a decade ago Florida Hospital began working with the Disney Corporation to create a groundbreaking facility that would showcase the model of health care for the twenty-first century and stay on the cutting edge of medical technology as it develops. A team of medical experts, industry leaders, and health-care futurists designed and built a whole-person health hospital named Celebration Health located in Disney's town of Celebration, Florida. Since opening its doors in 1997, Celebration Health has been awarded the Premier Patient Services Innovator Award as "The Model for Health-Care Delivery in the 21st Century."

When Dr. Lydia Parmele, the first female physician in the state of Florida, and her medical team opened Florida Hospital in 1908, their goal was to create a healing environment where they not only treated illness but also provided the support and education necessary to help patients achieve mental, physical, spiritual, and social health—or, simply put, whole-person health.

The lifestyle advocated by Florida Hospital founders remains central to carrying out that mission today. Patients learn how to reduce the risk of disease through healthy lifestyle choices, and they are encouraged to use natural remedies such as fresh air, sunshine, water, rest, nutrition, exercise, outlook, faith, and interpersonal relationships.

Today, Florida Hospital:

- Is ranked by the American Hospital Association as number one in the nation for inpatient admissions

- Is the largest provider of Medicare services in the country

- Performs the most heart procedures each year, making the number one hospital the leader in fighting America's number one killer—heart disease

- Operates many nationally recognized centers of excellence including Cardiology, Cancer, Orthopedics, Neurology & Neurosurgery, Digestive Disorders, and Minimally Invasive Surgery

- Is, according to *Fit Pregnancy* magazine, one of the "Top 10 Best Places in the Country to Have a Baby"

For more information about Florida Hospital and whole-person health products including books, music, videos, conferences, seminars, and other resources, please contact:

Florida Hospital Publishing
683 Winyah Drive, Orlando, FL 32803
Phone: 407-303-7711 • Fax: 407-303-1818
Email: healthproducts@flhosp.org
www.FloridaHospital.com • www.CreationHealth.com

VISIT
www.FORGIVETOLIVE.NET

Tell your story!

Did you have a "grievance story" that *Forgive to Live* helped you forgive for good? Come to **ForgiveToLive.net** to tell us your story. It could be seen by millions in Dr. Dick Tibbits future books and website. Most importantly, it will inspire others to learn how to *Forgive to Live*.

AT FORGIVETOLIVE.NET YOU CAN:

- Share your story
- Take the *Forgiveness Journey Quiz*
- Watch video clips
- Sign up for a free newsletter
- Learn how to become a certified *Forgive to Live* coach
- Order the new *Forgive to Live* video and other resources

Dr. Dick Tibbits is available to speak for your business, hospital, church or university. For more information about booking Dr. Tibbits visit *www.ForgiveToLive.net.*